Contents

Preface

The Sport and Exercise Psychology Section of The British Psychological Society officially came into being in April 1993 in Blackpool, though its anticipatory activities had started nearly two years earlier. It has so far organized five successful symposia, one jointly with the Psychology of Women Section, and two satellite workshops on different facets of sport and exercise, with special emphasis on what psychology can contribute to success.

The proceedings of the Section's most recent satellite workshop on Exercise Addiction, held on 31 March 1995 in Brighton, just before the BPS Annual Conference, are its first publication. BPS satellite workshops were largely the brain child of Professor Vicky Bruce, and have given the Section the opportunity to discuss work in progress and new ideas, as well as to survey the state of the art.

Exercise addiction is one of those interesting subjects which appears to be "media driven", but in fact has a long substantive history, in this case going back at least to Glasser's book on *Positive Addiction* in 1925. It has only fairly recently become recognized outside the specialist psychophysiological and clinical fields, partly under the stimulus of the discovery of "endorphins", the body's own opiate-like substances, and partly because of great public interest in keeping fit, (see e.g. N. Hawkes, *Times Newspaper*, 24 October 1994, p.16). As a result it is enjoying a research revival, which it is hoped this publication will help to enhance.

The effects of moderate physical exercise are of course mostly beneficial, and the underlying mechanisms whereby it can become obsessive or compulsive and behave like an addiction, are unclear; endorphin release remains a popular candidate, though it is unlikely to be the only mechanism.

A workshop with mixed participants of established and aspiring research workers and practitioners turned out to be an ideal format. The order of the contributions is, as it was at the meeting, informal and varied rather than strictly logical, in the hope that it will make a lively presentation. The major theories, facts and outstanding problems about exercise addiction – of which of course there are plenty – are described; the most important are discussed in some detail and are illustrated by empirical results and case histories.

Comments from members of the Section and other readers would be much appreciated. We are all indebted to Professor John Whiting for an excellent submission "bid" which set the scene for the workshop, The British Psychological Society's desk-top publishing team for producing a professional publication, Mrs Betty Cody for organizing the nuts and bolts of the workshop meeting and Miss Alison Dewey for her help.

H.S

List of Contributors

Professor John Annett
Department of Psychology, University of Warwick, Coventry CV4 7AL

Dr Peter J. Clough
Department of Psychology, University of Hull, Hull HU6 7RX

Dr Ian Cockerill
School of Sport and Exercise Sciences, University of Birmingham
PO Box 363, Birmingham B15 2TT

Rhonda Cohen
Barnet College, Russell Lane, Whetstone, London N20

Dr Barry Cripps
Riverside Cottage, Old Mill Crossing, Staverton, Totnes, Devon TQ9 6PD

Professor Craig Hall
Faculty of Kinesiology, University of Western Ontario, London,
Canada N6A 3K7

Mr Nick LeBoutillier
School of Psychology, Middlesex University, Queensway, Enfield EN3 4SF

Dr Konstantinos S. Loumidis
Department of Clinical Psychology, Withington Hospital,
West Didsbury, Manchester M20 8LR

Lisa Robertshaw
Department of Psychology, University of Hull, Hull HU6 7RX

Dr Hillary Roxborough
Department of Clinical Psychology, University of Manchester,
Rawnsley Building, Manchester Royal Infirmay, Manchester M13 9WL

Carole L. Seheult
Sport Psychology, University of Sunderland, Sunderland SR1 3SD

Dr David F. Sewell
Department of Psychology, University of Hull, Hull HU6 7RX

Professor Hannah Steinberg
School of Psychology, Middlesex University, Queensway, Enfield EN3 4SF

Professor Elizabeth A. Sykes
School of Psychology, Middlesex University, Queensway, Enfield EN3 4SF

Dr David Veale
Grovelands Priory Hospital, The Bourne, Southgate, London N14 6RA

Does Primary Exercise Dependence Really Exist?

David Veale

In a previous review, I tried to distinguish between clinical exercise dependence that is secondary to an eating disorder and primary exercise dependence where the motivation to exercise is more complex (de Coverly Veale, 1987). It is well known to clinicians that eating disorder patients may use exercise as an alternative to dieting, vomiting or laxative abuse, and sometimes the preoccupation with exercise becomes the dominant clinical feature. However, careful interviewing will tend to reveal other symptoms, such as a morbid fear of fatness.

There are very few exercise-dependent patients who seek treatment and my clinical impression is that patients with secondary exercise dependence are far more common than those with primary dependence. Their problems are also more severe as they are likely to be underweight and malnourished and therefore more likely to have physical injuries or illnesses. The focus of my paper is on individuals who have primary exercise dependence.

I want to consider three questions:

1) Does it really exist other than in a few case reports? Even these cases have not had a standardized diagnostic interview and are open to debate.

2) Does an eating disorder emerge after the exercise has subsided, as none of the cases have ever been followed up?

3) Can exercise dependence be properly distinguished from an over-training syndrome (Veale, 1991)?

A syndrome of primary exercise dependence has not been clinically validated and there is no recognition of it as a diagnostic category in either ICD-10 (World Health Organization, 1994) or DSM-IV (American Psychiatric Association, 1994). Psychologists on this side of the Atlantic are not keen on diagnostic categories and prefer models that are based upon a continuum. A continuum undoubtedly occurs in exercise dependence as in all forms of psychopathology but both models are useful. Categorical models have a pragmatic value as well as medico-legal and other uses. In general, individuals only seek help from clinicians when they reach the extreme end of the spectrum – for example if they are sufficiently distressed or handicapped in their health, family, social or occupational functioning. A clinical definition of exercise dependence would assist in its recognition by physicians and stimulate further research into motivation. I offer the following updated operational criteria which are in the style of DSM-IV or ICD-10 (see Table 1). They are based upon my clinical experience and a self-report measure of exercise dependence.

Table 1: Operational diagnostic criteria for "primary" exercise dependence

1. Preoccupation with exercise which has become stereotyped and routine.
2. Significant withdrawal symptoms in the absence of exercise (for example, mood swings, irritability, insomnia).
3. The preoccupation causes clinically significant distress or impairment in their physical, social, occupational or other important areas of functioning.
4. The preoccupation with exercise is not better accounted for by another mental disorder (e.g. as a means of losing weight or controlling calorie intake as in an eating disorder).

Individuals with primary exercise dependence do not tend to seek psychological help and are not generally referred to mental health specialists. This suggests that such individuals may: a) not be sufficiently distressed or handicapped in their physical health, family, social or occupational functioning; or b) deny that they have a problem or are "somatizing" their emotional distress; or c) have no confidence in the help that might be offered or even recognize that help could be available.

I have myself interviewed very few cases, despite having an interest in this area over the past eight years. I can only conclude that most of the time such individuals function reasonably well. Unlike a drug, there is never any shortage of exercise. Sometimes they overdose in the sense that they over-train and this leads them to experience chronic fatigue. In general, however, they adapt to their environment. For example, they may remain single or adopt partners who put up with their preoccupation. They tend to find employment that is physically demanding. They do not believe they have a problem because they have adapted their life to fit in with exercise but they remain vulnerable to cessation of exercise. They might have brief emotional crises if they have physical injuries and attend sports clinics and are advised to rest or reduce the intensity of the training. Informal talks with sports physicians suggest that such patients have great difficulty in complying with such advice and their recovery from a physical injury is prolonged. They do not however refer them on to a liaison psychiatrist or a sports psychologist. Occasionally they come to the attention of doctors when they continue to exercise through fevers or other illnesses and develop symptoms of chronic fatigue. Alternatively the patient may stop exercising but have a brief mood disorder during the enforced rest and withdrawal from exercise.

In summary, I believe primary exercise does exist but it is rare. There are probably many more cases with minor problems who have adapted their life to fit in with them and who never present. I will describe one case I have interviewed some time ago who would easily fulfil my operational definition and whom I would consider as a good example of "primary exercise dependence". I was able to use a standardized interview with her and hope to try to follow her up to see if she has ever developed an eating disorder.

She was a 27-year-old single unemployed woman who was a graduate in recreation management. She had responded to an advertisement in a local sports club requesting volunteers for a study of people who considered themselves addicted to exercise. She had not previously sought help for any emotional or behavioural problem related to her exercise. She was training to be a marathon runner and had a personal best time of 2 hours 40 minutes. Her weekly routine consisted of cycling 15 miles a day and twice-daily runs except on Sundays (average 14 miles) and Wednesdays (10 miles). She also did weight training twice a week.

When I saw her, the total amount of her running was not excessive but she had no other interests in life. She described her running as a compulsion ("I've got to do it"). She would experience withdrawal symptoms consisting of depressed mood, insomnia, restlessness, and indecisiveness when she had been forced to reduce her training because of an injury. She had once taken two overdoses in five days when she was withdrawing. She had presented to the Casualty Department but had not received any psychiatric help. She described her aims in life as "to run till I die" and to represent her country in the Olympics. One of the most striking aspects of her history was that she continued to exercise through back pain. On one occasion, she had run a marathon with a fever from German measles; on another occasion when she had a fever she had stopped after 16 miles. She had lost her partner because of her exercise and there were frequent arguments with her family about the amount of time she was spending exercising and the damage to her health. She did not work because it interfered with her training.

I used a standardized psychiatric interview which is divided into two parts (Goldberg et al., 1970). The first part is a systematic enquiry of any psychiatric symptoms which the patient may have experienced in the preceding week. The symptoms are rated on a five-point scale according to frequency and severity and are grouped in the following order: somatic symptoms, fatigue, sleep disturbance, irritability, lack of concentration, depression, anxiety, phobias, obsessions and depersonalisation. In the second section of the schedule, the interviewer rates the manifest abnormalities during the interview on 12 five-point scales. These are retardation, suspiciousness, histrionic behaviour, depression, anxiety, elation, flattened affect, excessive concern with bodily function, delusions, hallucinations and cognitive impairment. The patient had no overt psychiatric disorder and only scored highly on the item for "fatigue". She scored 14 on the Eating Attitudes Test (the normal cut-off score is 20 for an eating disorder). I also interviewed her with a structured schedule for eating disorders. Many athletes are extremely careful about their diet as leanness can improve performance. There was some concern about her weight and appearance as she tended to view herself as being too fat for a runner. She tended to skip lunch, was vegetarian and was careful about what she ate but she did not have a diagnosable eating disorder. She had a normal biochemistry, full blood count, and hormonal levels. Her periods were normal and she weighed 54kg.

Interestingly, there was a family history of depression in her mother and she herself had a past psychiatric history of depression at the age of 18. Her exercise could be considered as a means of preventing a recurrence of her mood disorder at the expense of her physical wellbeing. There is some evidence for exercise in the regulation of mood but against this is that overtraining in athletes may itself lead to mood disorders (Morgan et al., 1988) and upset this delicate balance.

The question is whether a clinical syndrome of primary exercise dependence requires further exploration in a clinical study that identifies individuals who are exercise dependent and who do not have an overt eating disorder. A self-report measure of exercise dependence is currently being developed (Ogden et al., 1994). The Exercise Dependence Questionnaire consists of 29 items and eight factors: interference with social or family life, positive reward, withdrawal symptoms, exercise for weight control, insight into problem, exercise for social reasons, exercise for health reasons and stereotyped behaviour. The questionnaire has also been validated against the Eating Attitudes Test and the Profile of Mood States. Those subjects who scored more than 20 on the EAT reported significantly higher scores on the total EDQ score and on all factors except "exercise for social reasons" and "exercise for health reasons". It is planned to validate the questionnaire in a second population before it is published.

The Exercise Dependence Questionnaire (Ogden et al., 1994) and the 26-item Eating Attitudes Test (Garner and Garfinkel, 1979) could be used to explore this question by identifying four groups of individuals from a population of subjects who exercise regularly:

(1) High EAT, High ED;
(2) High EAT, Low ED;
(3) Low EAT, Low ED;
(4) Low EAT, High ED.

A sample from each category could then be interviewed blind using a standardized diagnostic interview for DSM–IV to determine the various diagnoses and characteristics of each group. A more detailed structured eating disorder interview may also be required to validate the EAT in such a population, as some people will argue that such individuals have a "hidden" eating disorder which would not be picked up on the EAT. In this regard in-depth questioning is required to reveal the motivation for exercise, whether the individual (or a close relative) considers that they are distressed by their exercise, whether the patient is handicapped in health, social or occupational functioning and whether they have considered requesting help. The EAT-26 is a screening inventory and has a cut-off score of 20 for a probable diagnosis of an eating disorder. The Exercise Dependence Questionnaire does not yet have a cut-off score as it has not been clinically validated and so it will be necessary to interview a range of higher scores and perform the analysis to determine the best cut-off. It may also be necessary to determine whether the individual has an over-training syndrome which might further complicate the picture.

Such studies present considerable logistical difficulties as recruiting individuals can only be done by appeals to the media. Respondents are likely to be based all over the country and some interviews may need to take place by telephone.

References

American Psychiatric Association (1994). *Diagnostic and statistical manual of mental disorders* (4th edition). Washington, DC: American Psychiatric Association

Garner, D.M. and Garfinkel, P.E. (1979). The Eating Attitudes Test: an index of the symptoms of anorexia nervosa. *Psychological Medicine, 9,* 273-279.

Morgan, W.P., Costill, D.L, Flynn, M.G., Raglin, J. and O'Connor, P.J. (1988). Mood disturbance following increased training in swimmers. *Medicine and Science in Sports and Exercise, 20,* 408-414.

Ogden, J., Veale, D.M.W. and Summers, Z. (1994). *The Exercise Dependence Questionnaire.* Presented at European Congress of Behavioural and Cognitive Psychotherapy, London (submitted for publication).

De Coverly Veale, D.M.W. (1987). Exercise dependence. *British Journal of Addiction, 82, 735-740.*

Veale, D.M.W. (1991). Psychological aspects of staleness and dependence on exercise. *International Journal on Sports Medicine, 12 (Supp. 1),* S19-22.

World Health Organization (1994). The ICD-10 classification of mental and behavioural disorders. Geneva: World Health Organization.

Exercise Addiction: Indirect Measures of 'Endorphins'?

Hannah Steinberg, Elizabeth A. Sykes and Nick LeBoutillier

The concept of "addiction", or the milder term "dependence", is usually associated with drugs, especially opiates, though in recent years we have become accustomed to hearing about addiction to gambling, food (including, apparently, carrots – Cerny and Cerny, 1992), shopping, computers, and so forth. Exercise addiction is still a controversial concept, but as a general shorthand it can be defined as the inability to spend any length of time without exercise. No precise information is available, but it is usually regarded as affecting only a tiny proportion of the millions who exercise. It has been suggested that there are strong links with eating disorders (e.g. Huebner, 1993; Veale, 1987). Terms such as compulsive exercise, obligatory exercise and excessive exercise are also often used, and running seems to be the form of exercise most studied.

Although the idea of exercise addiction is not new, the discovery of endorphins, the body's own opiate-like substances, 20 years ago (Hughes et al., 1975) gave it a great boost when it was found that during and after vigorous physical exercise – and other forms of stress – these endogenous opioid peptides, notably beta-endorphin, are released into the bloodstream where they could be measured (see, for example, reviews by Steinberg and Sykes, 1985 and Steinberg et al., 1990).

Endorphins have been held at least partly responsible for several central effects of exercise, for example increased pain tolerance, favourable moods, including feelings of calmness (Allen and Coen, 1987) and, at the other extreme, euphoria, especially due to the "runner's high", and perhaps to other enjoyable activities (Hawkes, 1992).

Direct measurement of endorphins in the living brain is not yet possible, and it seems that major technical advances in, for example, scanning would be needed to make it so. Measurements post mortem in the brains of exercised laboratory animals make it seem unlikely that endorphin concentrations in brain and blood are closely related, though increases in brain endorphins over unexercised controls have usually been found (e.g. Blake et al., 1984), and this also seems to be the case if human cerebrospinal fluid (CSF) concentrations are measured (e.g. Hoffman et al., 1990).

For the time being one therefore has to content oneself with indirect evidence and analogies, and what follows is an attempt to link endorphins and exercise addiction in this way.

We start from evidence that "endorphins" ("endogenous morphines") are released into the bloodstream by exercise of varying intensity, and that if they are administered externally, e.g. by intravenous injection, they are "addictive" much as are opiate drugs, that is they can induce a withdrawal syndrome, tolerance and "craving", which is relieved by resuming administration. Many hormonal, cardiovascular and other physiological systems are of course involved in exercise as well, especially "stress hormones" such as prolactin and noradrenaline, and the detailed relationships between these systems and the endorphin system are likely to be extremely complex (e.g. Farrell et al., 1986; Grossman, 1988). Grossman et al. (1984) have suggested that exercise-induced activation of the endogenous opioid system may regulate and possibly damp down the secretion of several of the stress hormones during and after exercise.

If the central effects of exercise are indeed related to endorphin release, then one would expect that various behavioural criteria of the similarity of their actions to opiate drugs should be met.

Five years ago Steinberg et al. (1990) proposed four minimal criteria which would be consistent with the view that mechanisms underlying the psychological effects of physical exercise and especially exercise addiction are endorphin related, and indeed that physical exercise has opiate-like effects.

Such a state of affairs would have far reaching consequences. For example, opiate addicts being detoxified with the "milder" substitute opiate drug methadone could instead be given the opportunity of making their own opiate substitute by running or other exercise (e.g. Thoren et al., 1990; Steinberg 1993).

We have now expanded these criteria, and suggest the following:

The activity should be pleasurable and thus have reward value and lead to repetition. There is now a large literature showing that even single bouts of vigorous exercise can reduce mild anxiety and depression and induce positive moods and general feelings of wellbeing in a majority of subjects (e.g. Biddle and Mutrie, 1991; Janal et al., 1984; Plante and Rodin, 1990; Seraganian, 1993; Steinberg et al., 1994). Interesting support for the "endorphin hypothesis" appears in a recent personal account of depression by a distinguished biologist (Wolpert, 1995). It would hardly be ethical to try to induce human exercise addiction experimentally, but it is of interest that there seems to be a widespread need for exercise, so that even laboratory rodents seek out opportunities for increased activity. It has been reported that rats will voluntarily cover as much as 7km per night using an activity wheel (Shyu et al., 1982). Most investigations using human subjects seem to report improved moods, unless the exercise is short and intense (Steptoe and Bolton, 1988) but without necessarily a qualitatively different "high" (Morris et al., 1990a), the incidence of which has been reported to be confined to only a proportion of runners (Glasser, 1976). It is also possible that there are other more subtle benefits such as improved creative thinking which have been less studied but may be very rewarding to some people (Gondola, 1986; Steinberg et al., 1995; Wagemaker and Goldstein, 1980; Sachs and Buffone, 1985).

The activity should become excessive and compulsive. Descriptive evidence, including interviews, case histories and semi-popular articles (e.g. Hawkes, 1994) give the impression that compulsive exercising is perhaps commoner among the general population than is officially conceded, let alone among those competing in *élite* sport. As far as we know, no exact figures are available.

Pain thresholds should be raised. There is now a large, if scattered, literature on exercise raising pain thresholds, as indeed do other forms of stress, though the relationship with endorphins does not appear to be straightforward (Droste et al., 1991). The raised pain threshold may be one of the reasons why top athletes can keep going when others would succumb to pain (Black et al., 1979). It has been suggested that they can regulate their own endorphin release to a fine balance, so as to dampen down pain due to exercise but not so much that they ignore injury and the possibility of permanent damage (Panksepp, 1986). There is also evidence that the pain-relieving effects of acupuncture may work via the mobilization of endorphins (e.g. Thoren et al., 1990).

Withdrawal symptoms should occur. If opiate addicts are abruptly deprived of their accustomed drugs, they are apt to experience a "withdrawal syndrome" which can be violent and distressing ("cold turkey"). However, withdrawal from accustomed exercise is difficult to study experimentally, since regular exercisers do not readily give up their exercise temporarily for the sake of an experiment; only the less committed will, thus biasing the sample.

Most of the few investigations reported appear therefore to have had withdrawals only a few days long (e.g. Baekeland, 1970), though Thaxton et al.'s 1982 study showed that even one day's abstinence from running led to bouts of increased depression and increased galvanic skin reponse (GSR) in regular runners. Morris et al. (1990b) were able to report the effects of two weeks' deprivation from running in habitual runners, who were paid not to run. Significant increases in anxiety, depression, general malaise and symptoms of ill health occurred which subsided soon after running was reinstated (see Figure 1). Compared with "cold turkey", the syndrome was however relatively mild.

Opiate antagonists should oppose the psychological effects of exercise. Opiate antagonists such as nalorphine and naloxone have mostly been found to counteract exercise-induced positive moods and to induce mild dysphoria on their own; the findings are however not consistent and the dose and method of administration of the drugs seems to be important (see e.g. Steinberg and Sykes, 1985). Exercise-induced pain sensitivity can often be abolished by naloxone (e.g. Janal et al., 1984; Haier et al., 1981; Shyu et al., 1982) though precisely how endogenous opioids are involved in pain relief remains unclear (e.g. Akil et al., 1984; Melzack and Wall, 1991). Because of the practical problems of measuring endorphins, responses to antagonists are among the most important criteria.

Morris et al. (1990c) have obtained relevant results with naloxone, not with exercise but by using a stressful task with volunteers, with measures of heart rate and systolic and diastolic blood pressure to assess effects. The stressful task (a computerized version of the Stroop test) produced increases in all three measures in control subjects, but naloxone-treated subjects showed exaggerated pulse rate responses, while blood pressure, plasma adrenaline and noradrenaline and subjective

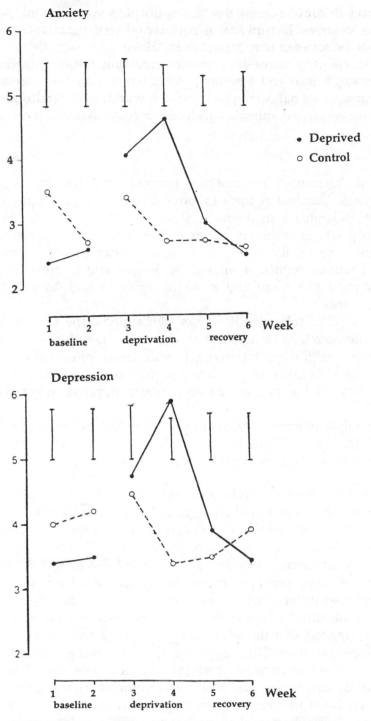

Figure 1. Withdrawal from running - increases in mean scores on Zung Activity and Depression scales. Bars show SED's for comparing groups on each occasion. The difference between the deprived and control groups was statistically significant only after the second week of deprivation and was not significant when running was resumed (After Morris et al., 1990c, reprinted by kind permission of Elsevier Science Inc.).

anxiety were unaffected. This suggests that the endorphin system is involved in the pulse rate response to stress. In different experimental settings blood pressure has also been reported to be affected (e.g. Farrell et al., 1986).

Perhaps the most impressive experiments involving opiate antagonists come from laboratory mice (Christie and Cheshire, 1982) which had been accustomed to swimming. Administration of naloxone precipitated a withdrawal syndrome similar to that precipitated in non-exercised animals which had become dependent on morphine.

Tolerance

The development of "tolerance" is a complex process, and the term is used in at least two major senses. The first is for a favourable effect, for example, when it is said that a patient "tolerates a medicine well which often has side effects". The second sense, appropriate to addiction, refers to the fact that it has become necessary to increase the dose of, for example, an opiate drug to obtain the effect or effects previously obtained with a smaller dose. Kagen and Squires (1985) report that many joggers must run more and more in order to feel "right", that is, to achieve their stable state.

This second kind of tolerance itself has two aspects: the original dose may now produce less intense effects or no effect at all, and/or the effects may now be of shorter duration than originally. Intertwined with these phenomena is a third, which is whether a drug is taken to produce a super-normal effect, as in a "high", or merely to restore what has become an abnormally negative effect, as in withdrawal, to "normal".

All this can apply *mutatis mutandis* to physical exercise, though tolerance as such seems not to have been much investigated, possibly because this would be highly labour intensive, though the literature on "training" contains relevant information.

Recently we have, with Nicholls, Ramlakhan and Moss (submitted), found a surprising difference between mood changes in beginner and advanced exercisers before and after a weekly aerobics class (preliminary report in Steinberg and Sykes, 1993).

Positive moods as measured by an adjective check-list greatly increased after both kinds of aerobics class, and negative moods decreased. However, before the class there was a marked difference between the two groups: the advanced group's mood was relatively negative, whereas the beginners' was predominantly positive (see Figure 2); this suggests that the advanced group may have become "tolerant" and needed their exercise more than beginners. On all these grounds the "endorphin" hypothesis of physical exercise is at least tenable (see e.g. Weinberg and Gould, 1995). Recently also there has been great interest in the phenomenon of "overtraining" which leads to "burnout" and possible impairment of the immune system. (e.g. Morgan, 1979; Sharp and Parry-Billings, 1992). This is close to exercise addiction but not identical, since it refers primarily to competitive athletes being coached for events rather than to the general population exercising in their own time. Dishman (1988) comments that "overtraining" in athletes involves a paradox because many of the beneficial effects known to accompany an exercise programme are reversed in the overtrained athlete.

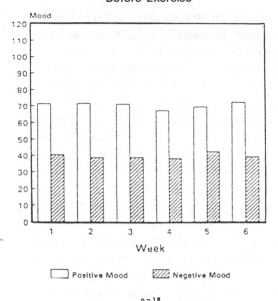

Beginner Exercisers
Before Exercise

☐ Positive Mood   ▨ Negative Mood

n – 18
Positive mood SEMs: 2.96 to 4.16
Negative mood SEMs: 2.52 to 3.46

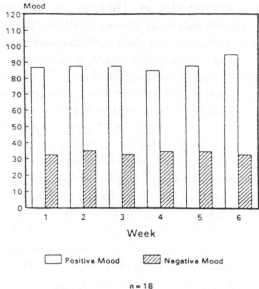

Beginner Exercisers
After Exercise

☐ Positive Mood   ▨ Negative Mood

n = 18
Positive mood SEMs: 2.28 to 3.46
Negative mood SEMs: 1.28 to 2.78

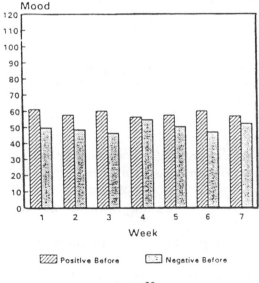

Advanced Exercisers
Before Exercise

▨ Positive Before   ▧ Negative Before

n = 20
Positive mood SEMs: 2.85 to 3.86
Negative mood SEMs: 3.04 to 5.17

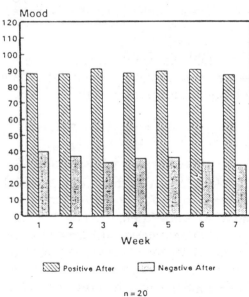

Advanced Exercisers
After Exercise

▨ Positive After   ☐ Negative After

n = 20
Positive mood SEMs: 4.32 to 5.12
Negative mood SEMs: 1.96 to 3.39

Figure 2. Mood changes in beginner and advanced exercisers - overall mood is enhanced in both groups, but the advanced group's pre-exercise mood is more negative than that of the beginners, though post-exercise scores are identical in both groups. This suggests that the advanced group "needed" their exercise more than the beginners. (Data after Steinberg, Nicholls, Sykes, Ramlakhan, Moss and LeBoutillier (submitted) and Steinberg and Sykes, 1993, reprinted by kind permission of S. Roderer Verlag.)

Among common symptoms, he lists increases in resting and exercise heart rates, increases in resting and exercise blood pressure, decreases in maximal aerobic power, increases in biochemical stress markers, decreased libido and appetite, weight loss, sleep disturbances, and so forth. Psychological effects include mood disturbances. It would seem likely that "overtraining" though not often explicitly mentioned in relation to exercise addiction also applies to exercise addicts.

Finally what about other "non-drug" addictions already mentioned, such as gambling, food (Huebner, 1993), computers, shopping, sex? Although little in the way of hard data seems to be available, it is possible that they involve sufficient stress for endorphin release to play a part; for example, some computer games have been reported to lead to endorphin release (Ramesh, 1995). It would also be particularly interesting to discover if there is a likely common genetic involvement. It has recently been claimed that some individuals carry a defective gene which predisposes - no more - to addiction to alcohol and drugs, and perhaps to other compulsive behaviours as well. It is even possible that there will, after all, be evidence for an addictive personality type which hitherto has been but poorly supported.

It has been argued that human survival almost inescapably involves the need to become dependent on something. Our hunch is that exercise dependence may turn out to be one of the least noxious forms of dependence; the idea of "positive addiction" to exercise has been strongly put forward by some (e.g. Glasser, 1976; Kostrubala, 1976). Clearly more comparative research is urgently needed. Meanwhile the maxim derived from the Greeks, *nothing to excess*, is perhaps the best advice.

Acknowledgements

The help of the Wolfson Foundation and of Miss Alison Dewey is gratefully acknowledged.

References

Akil, H., Watson, S.J., Young, E. Lewis, M.E, Khachaturian, H. and Walker, J.M. (1984). Endogenous opioids: biology and function. *American Review of Neuroscience, 7*, 223-255.

Allen, M.E. and Coen, D. (1987). Naloxone blocking of running-induced mood changes. *Annals of Sports Medicine, 3*, 190-195.

Baekeland, F. (1970). Exercise deprivation: sleep and psychological reactions. *Archives of General Psychiatry, 22*, 365.

Biddle, S. and Mutrie, N. (1991). *Psychology of physical activity and exercise.* London: Springer

Black, J., Chesher, G.B. and Starmer, G.A. (1979). The painlessness of the long distance runner. *Medical Journal of Australia, 2*, 522-523.

Blake, M.J., Stein, E.A. and Vomachka, A.J. (1984). Effects of exercise training on brain opioid peptides and serum LH in female rats. *Peptides, 5*, 953-958.

Blumenthal, J.A., Rose, S. and Chang, J.L. (1985). Anorexia nervosa and exercise: implications from recent findings. *Sports Medicine, 2*, 237-247.

Cerny, L. and Cerny, K. (1992). Can carrots be addictive? An extraodinary form of drug dependence. *British Journal of Addiction, 87* 1195-1197.

Christie, M.J. and Chesher, G.B. (1982). Physical dependence on physiologically released endogenous opiates. *Life Sciences, 30* 1173-1177.

Dishman, R.K. (Ed.) (1988). *Exercise adherence: Its impact on public health.* Champaign, Illinois: Human Kinetic.

Droste, C., Greenlee, M.W., Schreck, M. and Roskamm, H. (1991). Experimental pain thresholds and plasma beta-endorphin levels during exercise. *Medicine and Science in Sport and Exercise, 23,* 3, 334-342.

Farrell, P.A., Gustafson, A.B., Garthwaite, T.L., Kalhoff, R.K., Cowley, Jr. A.W. and Morgan, W.P. (1986). Influence of endogenous opioids on the response of selected hormones to exercise in humans. *American Journal of Physiology, 6,* 1051-1057.

Glasser, W. (1976). *Positive addiction.* New York: Harper & Row.

Gondola, J.C. (1986). The enhancement of creativity through long and short term exercise programs. *Journal of Social Behaviour and Personality, 1,* 1, 77-82.

Grossman, A., Bouloux, P. and Price, P. (1984). The role of opioid peptides in the hormonal responses to acute exercise in man. *Clinical Science, 67,* 483-491.

Grossman, A. (1988). Opioids and stress in man. *Journal of Endocrinology, 119,* 377-381.

Haier, R.J., Quaid, K. and Mills, J.C. (1981). Naloxone alters pain and perception after jogging. *Psychiatry Research, 5,* 231-232.

Hawkes, C.H. (1992). Endorphins: the basis of pleasure. *Neurology, Neurosurgery and Psychiatry, 55,* 247-250.

Hawkes, N. (1994). Addicted to exercise. *The Times Newspaper,* 24 October 1994, p.16.

Hoffman, P., Terenius, L. and Thoren, P. (1990). Cerebrospinal fluid immunoreactive beta-endorphin concentration is increased by long-lasting voluntary exercise in the spontaneously hypertensive rat. *Regulatory Peptides, 28,* 233-9.

Huebner, H. (1993). *Endorphins, eating disorders and other addictive behaviours.* London: W.W. Norton.

Hughes, J., Smith, T.W., Kosterlitz, H.W., Fothergill, L.A., Morgan, J.A. and Morris, H.R. (1975). Identification of two related pentapeptides from the brain with potent opiate agonist activity. *Nature, 258,* 577-579.

Janal, M.N., Colt, E.W.D., Clark, W.C. and Glusman, M. (1984). Pain sensitivity mood and plasma endocrine levels in man following long-distance running: effects of naloxone. *Pain, 19,* 13-25.

Kagen, D.M., and Squires, R.L. (1985). Addictive aspects of physical exercise. *Journal of Sports Medicine, 25,* 227-237.

Kostrubala, T. (1976). *The joy of running.* Philadelphia: J.B.Lippincott.

Melzack, R. and Wall, P.D. (1991) *The challenge of pain* (4th edition). London: Penguin.

Morgan, W.P. (1979). Negative addiction in runners. *Physician and Sports-medicine, 7,* 57-70.

Morris, M., Salmon, P. and Steinberg, H. (1990a). The "runner's high": dimensions of mood states after running. *Proceedings of Sport, Health, Psychology & Exercise Symposium 1988,* Sports Council and HEA, pp.147-152.

Morris, M., Salmon, P., Steinberg, H., Sykes, E.A., Bouloux, P., Newbould, E., McLoughlin, L., Besser, G.N. and Grossman, A. (1990b). Endogenous opioids modulate the cardiovascular response to mental stress. *Psychoneuroendocrinology, 15,* 185-192.

Morris, M., Steinberg, H., Sykes, E.A. and Salmon, P. (1990c). Effects of temporary withdrawal from regular running. *Journal of Psychosomatic Research, 34*, 5, 493-500.

Panksepp, J. (1986). The neurochemistry of behaviour. *Annual Review of Psychology, 37*, 77-107.

Plante, T.G. and Rodin, J. (1990). Physical fitness and enhanced psychological health. *Current Psychology: Research and Review*, 9, 1, 3-24.

Ramesh, R. (1995). Children "drugged" by computer game's hidden messages. *The Sunday Times*, 8 October 1995.

Sachs, M.L. and Buffone, G.W. (Eds) (1985). *Running as therapy: An intergrated approach*. London: University of Nebraska Press.

Seraganian, P. (1993). *The influence of physical exercise on psychological processes*. Wiley: New York.

Sharp, C. and Parry-Billings, M. (1992). Can exercise damage your health? *New Scientist*, 15 August 1992, 33-37.

Shyu, B.C., Andersson, S.A. and Thoren, P. (1982). Endorphin mediated increase in pain threshold induced by long-lasting exercise in rats. Life Sciences, 30, 883-890.

Steinberg, H. and Sykes, E.A. (1985). Introduction to symposium on endorphins and behavioural processes: review of literature on endorphins and exercise. *Pharmacology, Biochemistry and Behavaviour, 23*, 857-862.

Steinberg, H., Sykes, E.A. and Morris, M. (1990). Exercise addiction: the opiate connection. In *Proceedings of Sport, Health, Psychology & Exercise Symposium 1988*. Sports Council and HEA, pp.161-166.

Steinberg, H. (1993). Habit Forming: Hannah Steinberg on smoking, drugs and the young, (review of three books). *Times Educational Supplement*, 12 February 1993.

Steinberg, H. and Sykes, E.A. (1993). Mood enhancement through physical exercise - introduction to workshop on health, sport and physical exercise. In H. Schroder, K. Reschke, M. Johnston, and S. Maes (Eds) *Health Psychology, Potential in Diversity*, pp.204-209. Regensburg: S. Roder Verlag.

Steinberg, H., Nicholls, B., Sykes, E.A., Ramlakhan, N., Moss, T. and LeBoutillier, N. (1995, in press). Weekly exercise reinstates favourable mood (submitted).

Steptoe, A., and Bolton, J. (1988). The short term influence of high and low intensity physical exercise on mood. *Psychology and Health, 2*, 91-106.

Sykes, E.A., LeBoutillier, N., Moss, T. and Steinberg, H. (1994). Dissociation between improvement of mood and creativity following exercise (in press).

Thaxton, L. (1982). Physiological and psychological effects of short-term exercise addiction on habitual runners. *Journal of Sport Psychology, 4*, 73-80.

Thoren, P., Floras, J.S. and Hoffman, P. (1990). Endorphins and exercise physiological mechanisms and clinical implications. *Medicine and Science in Sport and Exercise, 22, 4*, 417-428.

Veale, D.M. (1987). Exercise dependence. *British Journal of Addiction, 82*, 735-740.

Wagemaker, H. Jr and Goldstein, L. (1980) The runner's high. *Journal of Sports Medicine and Physical Fitness, 20*, 227-229.

Weinberg, R.S. and Gould, D. (1995). *Foundations of Sport and Exercise Psychology*. Human Kinetics: Champaign, Illinois.

Wolpert, L. (1995) Descent into darkness. *The Guardian Newspaper*, 17 August 1995.

3

The Motivational Function of Mental Imagery for Participation in Sport and Exercise

Craig R. Hall

A dependency on physical activity has been given a variety of labels in the research literature (e.g., addiction, obligatory, compulsive, excessive, perfectionism). While these terms are often vaguely defined and hastily measured, they all point to the fact that exercise can be harmful when engaged in excessively. Exercise addiction can be characterized by an excessive dominance of exercise in daily life and withdrawal symptoms if exercise is not possible. Addicts may exercise despite injury, at the expense of interpersonal relationships, to the detriment of their work, or with other consequences (see Coen and Ogles, 1993; Morgan, 1979; Yates, 1991).

Much of the research on exercise addiction has compared compulsive exercisers, especially runners, with groups that engage in other excessive activities. For example, Yates and her colleagues (Yates, 1987, 1991; Yates et al., 1983) propose that exercise addicts and anorexic women have some similar psychological reasons for their excessive activity (exercise or eating). They argue that extreme running and extreme dieting represent partially successful attempts to establish identity. Another focus of the exercise addiction research has been to assess the personality characteristics of the participants. It has been suggested that compulsive exercisers tend to exhibit perfectionism, high levels of anxiety, and obsessiveness (Coen and Ogles, 1993; Goldfarb and Plante, 1984).

These studies have provided some insight into the problem of exercise addiction, but much more attention needs to be given to this issue. Researchers have tended to primarily focus on initial motives for exercise participation, and reasons for adherence or discontinuation of exercise (e.g., Duncan et al., 1993; Kendzierski and Johnson, 1993).

Many recent exercise-adherence studies have investigated the utility of various theoretical models in explaining exercise participation. As Yordy and Lent (1993) point out, this work is important because it identifies promising predictors of exercise, encourages revision of useful models, promotes integration of findings across studies, and may aid in the development of interventions aimed at sedentary people or those who do not exercise at optimal levels. While this work is undoubtedly worthwhile, it generally fails to consider the end of the exercise participation continuum associated with addiction. One useful approach for examining the participation motivation of people addicted to exercise may be Bandura's (1986) global social-cognitive theory. Two major components of this theory are self-efficacy and outcome expectancy. Self-efficacy is a person's belief that he or she can perform a particular behaviour, while outcome expectancy is a person's estimate that a given behaviour will lead to certain outcomes. Self-efficacy and outcome expectancy can exist simultaneously in a person's mind prior to his or her undertaking any behaviour and, therefore, both can function as determinants of behavioural intention (see Maddux et al., 1986; Rodgers and Brawley, 1991). There are various ways these two variables may operate in exercise addiction. For example, individuals may believe they can still exercise despite being injured (self-efficacy), and may worry about being perceived as a failure if they don't exercise or cut back on the amount they exercise (outcome expectancy).

Self-efficacy can be derived from numerous sources including performance accomplishments, physiological arousal, verbal persuasion, and observing others. One other important source of efficacy is mental imagery. Feltz (1984) argues that "just mentally seeing oneself successfully performing the desired task is enough to convince the athlete that he or she has the ability to successfully execute the task" (p.193). There is also indirect evidence that imagery can influence outcome expectancy (Salmon et al., 1994). Consequently, imagery would seem to be a worthwhile variable to consider when investigating participation motivation as it relates to exercise addiction.

The motivational function of imagery

Paivio (1985) proposed a simple framework suggesting that imagery can have both a cognitive and motivational function in mediating motor behaviour, and that each function can operate either at a specific or general level. The cognitive function is essentially concerned with the practising of skills and general strategies of play through the use of imagery. Most of the mental practice research focuses on how imagery can improve the learning and enhance the performance of specific motor skills (see Feltz et al., 1988 and Hall et al., 1992 for reviews). The motivational function of imagery involves symbolically representing various behavioural situations. On a specific level, athletes can imagine a successful performance and the subsequent rewards. On a general level, imagery can represent both the physiological arousal and the emotional affect that may accompany performances. Researchers have only recently started to consider this function of imagery.

Salmon et al. (1994) investigated the motivational and cognitive use of imagery by soccer players. The Imagery Use Questionnaire for Soccer Players was administered to 362 players at national, provincial and local levels. This questionnaire was designed to assess imagery use in the four cells of Paivio's (1985) model (i.e. cognitive specific, cognitive general, motivational specific, and motivational general). They found that soccer players tend to use imagery more for its motivational function than its cognitive function. Furthermore, players responded with the highest ratings for the motivational general cell, suggesting that they use imagery to energize themselves to practice and play.

Given that imagery has a strong motivational function, we need to understand exactly how this function operates. It was argued by Salmon et al (1994) that imagery may encourage athletes to practice and play. Research by Hall, Toews et al. (1990) supports this point. They compared imagery practice to a control condition to determine whether imagining a laboratory motor task increased the amount and length of voluntary physical practice of the task. They found that the imagery group came into the laboratory more often to practice the motor task than the control group. There was also a trend for the imagery group to work longer when they did practice.

In addition to influencing practice behaviour, Hall, Rodgers et al. (1990) propose that "using imagery (for competitive purposes) may help keep athletes focused on their event, self-confident about their upcoming performance, and in control of their emotions and arousal level" (p.7). This possibility was investigated in recent studies we conducted with roller skaters (Moritz et al., 1995; Vadocz and Hall, 1995). Participants at the Junior North American Roller Skating Championships were given the Sport Imagery Questionnaire (SIQ; Hall et al., 1995), the Competitive State Anxiety Inventory – 2 (CSAI-2; Martens et al., 1990), and the State Sport Confidence Inventory (SSCI; Vealey, 1986). The SIQ was used to measure the functions of imagery proposed by Paivio (1985), the important ones for the present discussion being motivational specific, motivational general-arousal, and motivational general-affect. Table 1 provides examples of the types of items intended to measure each of these functions. The CSAI-2 was used to measure the skaters' cognitive state anxiety and somatic state anxiety. It also includes a self-confidence sub-scale.

Table 1. Examples of items in the Sport Imagery Questionnaire (SIQ)

Motivational specific	Motivational general-arousal	Motivational general-affect
I imagine myself winning a medal	I imagine the stress and anxiety associated with competing	I imagine myself being focused during a challenging situation
I imagine being interviewed as a champion	I imagine the excitement associated with competing	I imagine myself being mentally tough

The SSCI was also employed to assess sport confidence. Although the terms self-efficacy and self-confidence have often been used interchangeably, in this study self-confidence referred to an individual's overall belief in his or her sport ability. In contrast, self-efficacy usually refers to a belief in being able to execute successfully a very specific sport behaviour in order to produce a certain outcome. For example, a player may have a high degree of self-confidence in his or her ability to play ice hockey (sport self-confidence); however, he or she may not be very successful in scoring goals on a breakaway (sport self-efficacy).

Subjects completed the SIQ when registering for the competition. The SSCI and the CSAI-2 were administered to the athletes shortly before they competed. Several multiple regression analyses were conducted using either the SSCI scores or the CSAI-2 scores as the dependent variables, and the SIQ scores and other measures (e.g., imagery ability, age, gender, experience) as predictor variables. The best predictor of state sport confidence (SSCI scores and CSAI-2 self-confidence sub-scale scores) was the motivational general-affect function of imagery. The motivational general-arousal function of imagery predicted cognitive anxiety. These findings indicate that how athletes use imagery is related to how they perceive an upcoming performance. Top athletes tend to imagine themselves in control of the situation, being focused, confident and prepared.

The results of the research on imagery use by athletes seem clear. The more élite the athlete, the more he or she uses imagery. Furthermore, imagery is employed most for its motivational function. Athletes imagine the goals they want to achieve, such as being successful and winning. They use imagery to increase self-confidence and control arousal levels, and the more they use imagery, the more beneficial it seems to be.

The role of imagery in participation motivation for exercise

Given that imagery is a powerful motivator in sport, it is very possible that imagery operates in a similar fashion in exercise. People who are regular exercisers may often imagine themselves participating in their favourite forms of exercise. They probably imagine themselves enjoying their workouts and achieving their desired outcomes. How imagery might influence exercise participation is outlined by the model depicted in Figure 1.

This model obviously is based on Bandura's (1986) social-cognitive theory and the above research on imagery use by athletes. According to the model, exercise participation is influenced by self-confidence, including the related concept of self-efficacy, and by outcome expectancy. Imagery is a determinant of self-confidence, both directly, and indirectly through other variables such as anxiety. That is, by imagining themselves in the exercise situation, performing the way they want to perform, individuals become more self-confident. And by imagining themselves in control in the exercise setting, they moderate their anxiety levels and this, in turn, influences their self-confidence.

Outcome expectancy is considered to be the product of outcome likelihood (OL) and outcome value (OV) (Rodgers and Brawley, 1991). OL is simply how likely a person feels a particular outcome may be. OV represents the importance of the outcome in question to that person. In the case of some exercise participants, for example, it could be that they feel exercising will make them fit, and fitness is very important to them. Therefore, in this case both OL and OV will be combining to produce an outcome expectancy that encourages further exercise participation. Imagery probably influences OL more than OV. By imagining a given outcome such as successfully achieving some level of fitness, much like an élite athlete might imagine winning, a person may feel the likelihood of that outcome is greater.

Given that imagery is an important determinant of exercise participation, then excessive use of imagery may help foster exercise addiction. Two especially important aspects of the model for helping to explain how imagery use can become excessive are: a) the interaction between imagery ability and imagery use; and b) the feedback loop from outcome to imagery. Research by Rodgers et al. (1991) has demonstrated that imagery ability improves with imagery training. One of the variables

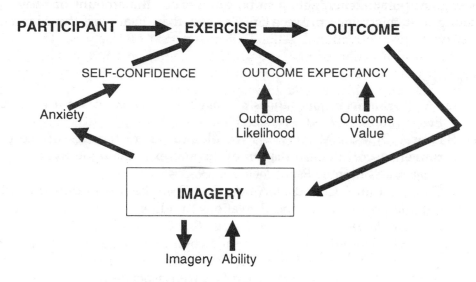

Figure 1. A model of participation motivation for exercise

examined in the imagery use studies involving the roller skaters (Moritz et al., 1995; Vadocz and Hall, 1995) was imagery ability. In these studies it was found that skaters scoring higher on imagery ability used imagery to a greater extent. Together these findings suggested that the more individuals use imagery, the better imagers they become, and the better imagers they become, the more likely they are to use imagery. Achieving a desired outcome previously imagined will also promote increased use of imagery, especially if the individual believes imagery may have been partially responsible for achieving that outcome. Many top athletes claim that you have to imagine yourself winning before it will become a reality. If you don't think you can win, you probably won't.

The advantage of the model being proposed here is that it makes some very specific predictions and these predictions are testable. Each of the variables assumed to influence exercise participation can be readily assessed. Instruments such as the SIQ could easily be adapted for measuring imagery use in exercise. Rodgers and Brawley (1991) have demonstrated how OV and OL can be conceptually and methodologically combined to assess outcome expectancy, and there are numerous instruments and approaches for measuring self-confidence and self-efficacy. Some of the relationships outlined in the model have been confirmed in sport settings (e.g., imagery use affects self-confidence and anxiety); they now need to be examined in the context of exercise.

From an applied standpoint, it is important to realize that the variables included in this model are, for the most part, socially learned. For example, through experience and persuasion an individual's perception of outcome likelihood can be influenced (Maddux et al., 1986), and through practice an individual's use of imagery will change (Rodgers et al., 1991). This makes it possible to include these variables in interventions. Given that imagery is an important determinant of exercise participation, then an intervention programme aimed at altering how people addicted to exercise imagine their participation and the outcomes they hope to achieve could prove beneficial. Another possibility might be to try and reduce the amount of imagery people are using, but this might prove more difficult than changing the content of their imagery.

References

Bandura, A. (1986). *Social foundations of thought and action. A social cognitive theory.* Englewood Cliffs, NJ: Prentice-Hall.

Coen, S.P. and Ogles, B.M. (1993). Psychological characteristics of the obligatory runner. A critical examination of the anorexia analogue hypothesis. *Journal of Sport and Exercise Psychology, 15,* 338-354.

Duncan, T.E., Duncan, S.C. and McAuley, E. (1993). The role of domain and gender-specific provisions of social relations in adherence to a prescribed exercise regimen. *Journal of Sport and Exercise Psychology, 15,* 220-231.

Feltz, D.L. (1984). Self-efficacy as a common cognitive mediator of athletic performance. In W.F. Straub and J.M. Williams (Eds) *Cognitive sport psychology* (pp.191-198). Lansing, NY: Sport Science Associates.

Feltz, D.L., Landers, D.M. and Becker, B.J. (1988). A revised meta-analysis of the mental practice literature on motor learning. In D. Druckman and J. Swets (Eds) *Enhancing human performance: Issues, theories and techniques* (pp. 1-65). Washington, DC: National Academy Press.

Goldfarb, L.A. and Plante, T.G. (1984). Fear of fat in runners: An examination of the connection between anorexia nervosa and distance running. *Psychological Reports, 55,* 296.

Hall, C., Buckolz, E. and Fishburne, G.J. (1992). Imagery and the acquisition of motor skills. *Canadian Journal of Sport Sciences, 17,* 19-27.

Hall, C. Mack, D. and Paivio, A. (1995). *Imagery use by athletes: the development of an imagery use by athletes questionnaire.* Paper presented at the annual meeting of the Canadian Society for Psychomotor Learning and Sports Psychology, Hamilton, Canada.

Hall, C., Rodgers, W. and Barr, K. (1990). The use of imagery by athletes in selected sports. *The Sport Psychologist, 4,* 1-10.

Hall, C., Toews, J. and Rodgers, W. (1990). Les aspects motivationnels de l'imagerie en activites motrices [The motivational function of imagery]. *Revue des Sciences et Téchniques des Activités physiques et sportives, 22,* 27-32.

Kendzierski, D. and Johnson, W. (1993). Excuses, excuses, excuses: A cognitive behavioral approach to exercise implementation. *Journal of Sport and Exercise Psychology, 15,* 207-219.

Maddux, J.E., Norton, L.W. and Stoltenberg, C.D. (1986). Self-efficacy expectancy, outcome expectancy and outcome value: Relative effects on behavioral intentions. *Journal of Personality and Social Psychology, 51,* 738-789.

Martens, R., Burton, D., Vealey, R.S., Bump, L.A. and Smith, D.E. (1990). Development and validation of the Competitive State Anxiety Inventory-2. In R. Martens, R.S. Vealey and D. Burton (Eds) *Competitive anxiety in sport* (pp.117-190). Champaign, IL: Human Kinetics.

Morgan, W.P. (1979). Negative addiction in runners. *The Physician and Sports Medicine, 7,* 57-70.

Moritz, S., Hall, C. and Martin, K. (1995). The relationship between self-confidence, mental imagery and performance. Manuscript submitted for publication.

Paivio, A. (1985). Cognitive and motivational functions of imagery in human performance. *Canadian Journal of Applied Sport Sciences, 10,* 22S-28.

Rodgers, W.M. and Brawley, L.R. (1991). The role of outcome expectancies in participation motivation. *Journal of Sport and Exercise Psychology, 13,* 411-427.

Rodgers, W., Hall, C. and Buckolz, E. (1991). The effect of an imagery training program on imagery ability, imagery use, and figure skating performance. *Journal of Applied Sport Psychology, 3,* 109-125.

Salmon, J., Hall, C. and Haslam, I. (1994). The use of imagery by soccer players. *Journal of Applied Sport Psychology, 6,* 116-133.

Vadocz, E. and Hall, C. (1995). The cognitive and motivational functions of imagery in the anxiety-performance relationship. Manuscript submitted for publication.

Vealey, R.S. (1986). Imagery training for performance enhancement. In J.M. Williams (Ed.) *Applied sport psychology: Personal growth to peak performance* (pp.209-234). Palo Alto, CA: Mayfield Publishing Company.

Yates, A. (1987). Eating disorders and long-distance running: The ascetic condition. *Integrated Psychiatry, 5,* 201-211.

Yates, A. (1991). *Compulsive exercise and the eating disorders: Toward an integrated theory of activity.* New York: Brunner/Mazel.

Yates, A., Leehey, K. and Shisslak, C.M. (1983). Running - an analogue of anorexia? *New England Journal of Medicine, 308,* 251-255.

Yordy, G.A. and Lent, R.W. (1993). Predicting aerobic exercise participation: Social cognitive, reasoned action, and planned behavior models. *Journal of Sport and Exercise Psychology, 15,* 363-374.

4

Exercise Addiction and Chronic Fatigue Syndrome: Case Study of a Mountain Biker

Barry Cripps

This case study follows the life of a young mountain biker, John, from the age of 19 when he came fifth in the national championships, through to the present time. It is a study of intense dedication to sport, over-training, physiological collapse, and subsequent improving recovery which is not yet complete.

> *In an attempt to understand people's motivation for extremely strenuous sports (i.e. marathon, triathlon), attention might be directed to the phenomenon of addiction to these types of exercises. Apparently, some people have become addicted to these activities, and their addiction provides an answer to the question why they take part. (Bakker, 1990)*

When we take up any sport, exercise or leisure activity, it is usually because of their intrinsic qualities and because we enjoy the feeling of participation and the benefits that exercise brings. The motivation for participation in sport and exercise could be seen to be on a continuum of no participation right through to obsessive, addictive participative behaviour. We call the addictive, obsessive end of the continuum, exercise addiction.

> *Exercise addiction is characterized by dependency on physical activity in one or more of its forms, and by withdrawal symptoms if participation is denied. Dependency manifests itself in an excessive dominance of exercise in everyday life, often to the detriment of other facets such as the family, social contacts or work. Withdrawal symptoms include, on the psychological front, feelings of nervousness, guilt, anxiety and lowered self-esteem and, on the physiological front, headaches and physical discomfort. (Whiting, 1994)*

This paper supports the psychological symptoms included above but adds the chronic fatigue syndrome to the physiological symptoms, suggesting that there may be a psychosomatic cause behind this severe physiological state. Whiting continues:

> *Addiction is to be distinguished from commitment which is based on a logical analysis of the benefits of exercise such as social contact, healthy lifestyle and (particularly in the case of sport participation) monetary rewards. Addiction as such represents the extreme of a continuum of exercise participation which can become obsessive.*

Steinberg et al. (1990) report that "regular physical exercise, especially running, can become compulsive, and this has been described as a form of dependence or addiction, similar to addiction to opiates and other drugs" (Glasser, 1976; Steinberg and Sykes, 1985; Veale, 1987a, 1987b). Steinberg and Sykes conclude that exercise addiction is probably less noxious than some other forms of compulsive behaviour and might be a viable substitute for them.

This case study, however, looks at an extremely severe case of exercise addiction, where the psychophysiological mechanisms got out of hand, as it were, and began to have deleterious effects on the subject's health and wellbeing. Whereas, according to Steinberg and Sykes, it has often been suggested that the beneficial effects of physical exercise on mental health can be partly explained by the increase in endorphins which accompanies energetic exercise, the "opiate connection" may also account for the compulsion to exercise or exercise addiction which can develop. This paper in no way purports to investigate or even to understand the opiate connection. It is however interesting that the underlying mechanisms which produce the runner's high may also be producing a chronic fatigue syndrome. Much more work is needed looking at both ends of the exercise continuum. Steinberg and Sykes (1985) support this view.

> It also depends on several analogies between effects of exercise and those of opiates: first, reports that exercise can produce a 'high', that is, emotional states of euphoria and enthusiasm, similar to states described after ingestion of opiates; secondly, findings that tolerance of pain increases after exercise, as after administration of opiates; and thirdly, the more general idea that exercise can, in many respects, behave like an addiction, similar to opiate addiction.

So, whereas superficially sport and exercise research may seem straightforward, the links between the brain and the body are so complex and interdependent that much further work will be needed to unravel their entanglement.

This paper, as part of the search towards enlightenment, is merely a report of the effects of over-training and, of course, interesting from the therapeutic point of view in that it suggests a positive way out of such an entanglement by therapists for subjects who may be addicted to exercise.

As well as considering possible psychobiological mechanisms, the paper considers the relationship between personality theory, physical exercise and exercise addiction. Pargman and Burgess (1976) report "a relative dearth of interest, information and application of theory dealing with exercise dependence exists. Moreover, a precise definition of this term has not been agreed upon. Motor and athletic educators appear to be concerned with individuals who cannot be motivated to attend classes, team practice or training sessions."

This paper is a case study looking at the other end of this continuum and asks questions about what happens to motivation for participation when an athlete over-trains.

Background

The subject of this case study, pseudonym John, began mountain biking at the age of 16. His exercise history in secondary school was very positive and included a mixture of squash and cross-country running. Aged 17, he joined a good local squash club and began to excel. After leaving school John went to a local college of further education and embarked on a leisure and recreation course which he passed easily with very little academic input. His comment about himself at that age is that he was "bright, brainy and well into sport". Sport made him popular among his peers and in 1989 he won his first mountain bike event. In mountain biking he soon rose up the ladder to become one of the top 10 British juniors. When he was riding he took risks and was reckless on his bike. He began to dedicate himself and cut himself off from what we would consider to be a normal social development of a post-teenager. He reports that life became very lonely, and he didn't feel that he particularly fitted in. Whereas he was very comfortable in taking part in sport, he was not particularly comfortable at parties with his peers. When he was 19 he was sponsored by a manufacturer and had a very reasonable first half of the season. He peaked early and took part in approximately 20 events throughout Europe. In 1992, when he was aged 20, he could only complete about seven or eight events during the whole of that season. He found competition very hard indeed, and reports that his body was "stressed out" at that time.

The next year, in 1992, John came fifth in the Nationals, and reports that it was the first event he felt good riding in: "I couldn't understand it, I felt my old self". Towards the end of 1992, however, his performances faded off again. By September 1992 John had established enough of a reputation to go to the World Championships in Canada. He says about that time that he knew he wouldn't do well, however. He fell off in the downhill event and was concussed. Before this he did not qualify in the cross-country event because he says that his fatigue interrupted so much that he only did one lap. During Christmas 1992, John felt that maybe he could improve his performance by changing his diet, and so he stopped eating dairy products and began to eat a lot of pasta, cereals and carbohydrates. The 1993 season went by with very little competition and with John feeling continually fatigued. He came to see me in the middle of 1994 and reported that he felt normal, but not like an athlete. He tried to eat a sensible diet, but occasionally binged on junk food. He had lost his motivation and felt that he didn't care at all for himself. He had stopped training properly and stopped doing a lot of stretching work which he enjoyed.

Exercise programme

John reported that his illness, i.e. his problem, began when he decided to "go for it" in 1990. He undertook a 16-week training programme devised by an exercise physiologist. The programme ran daily from Monday to Friday. Typical days were:

Monday	Turbo training plus road session
	Intervals: 5 minutes at pulse rate of 150
	5 minutes at pulse rate 125
	1 hour on the road, heart rate 135-150
Tuesday	Road
	2 hours cycling, heart rate 130-150

Wednesday	Turbo trainer
	Intervals: 8 at pulse rate 150
	5 at pulse rate 125
Thursday	2 hours mountain biking on rough terrain
Friday	Roadwork – 3 hours on road, heart rate 135-150
Saturday	Rest, swimming, reading
Sunday	Mountain biking on rough terrain
	3 hours mountain biking work on riding up the hills

The programme was graded but increased in intensity over 16 weeks.

Week 6 reads:

Monday	Road and turbo
	Intervals plus 1 hour on the road, pulse rate 140-155
Tuesday	Roadwork
	3 hours, pulse rate 130-155
Wednesday	Intervals, turbo: 10 at pulse rate 160
	5 at pulse rate 140
Thursday	Mountain biking, 3 hours off-road
Friday	Road session, 4 hours pulse rate 130-155
Saturday	Rest
Sunday	Mountain biking 3 hours steady

Week 14 reads:

Monday	Rest day
Tuesday	Road 3-4 hours, pulse rate 160
Wednesday	Mountain biking over rough terrain, 3 hours
Thursday	Turbo training
	Interval training at pulse rate 170
	Finish with swimming
Friday	Road 3-4 hours, pulse rate 165
Saturday	Mountain biking over rough terrain 3-4 hours, mid-high intensity
Sunday	Rest

The programme ran for 16 weeks and included a gradual build up and taper down towards the racing season. This would appear to be a fairly reasonable but strenuous programme for an athlete aged around 25-30. For someone aged 18-plus, however, it might be considered by exercise physiologists to be rather heavy. John reported that for the whole of this training period he was not recovering and consequently felt tired. His sleeping patterns were irregular and he often suffered from sore throats.

When he started competing around June 1990 he was trying hard but felt that his body had no power and that he was getting nowhere. Occasionally he reported that his heart was over-working and his pulse rate would shoot up when he was doing mild exercise. He felt that his pulse rate was over-working by about 40 beats. John went to a specialist in sports physiology who diagnosed chronic fatigue and advised him to take the rest of the 1990 season off. In 1991 he started a gradual build-up and at first everything seemed all right. His first race was hard and he pushed hard but felt that he wasn't getting anywhere. He finished fourth in one event, which was quite good, but felt that he could have done a lot better. Throughout the '91 and '92 seasons, for race after race he felt that it was hard work, and he rarely felt good at all during racing.

In 1992 he became seriously ill and suffered a high temperature for two weeks. His joints seized up and a doctor diagnosed summer flu. John couldn't move, however, and suffered high temperatures. When he recovered from this illness, he picked up a little and came fifth in the Nationals in 1992. He actually felt good with no training(!) and felt in relatively good shape. After the Nationals, the next weekend, he was expected to do well, but he went back to his old feelings of fatigue and reported that the race was such hard work, even though he came third. John went to Canada for the Worlds and was looking forward to it immensely, although he knew that he was not going to do well. He felt tired and that he needed a rest. He did not qualify for the cross country but was going OK in the downhill when he crashed badly while in twelfth place. He was concussed, dropped out, and his season finished.

In the 1992-3 season John went to a dietician who began to use iridology to cleanse his body systems. She told him he was allergic to wheat and the diet she put him on made him feel cleaner. His training in 1993 was going well although he was taking it easy, experiencing only the odd dry throat.

In the middle of the season he rode in a 100-mile race, and said he nearly died. His heart rate was high and he never really recovered from that ride for the rest of the season. He got the shakes and shivers, felt cold and his iron stores were low. He took iron supplements and appeared to improve and return to normal, so that he could come off the iron tablets. He felt his health was up and down and that he was deteriorating. At times he could hardly walk and felt completely wiped out even after 12 hours' sleep at night and two or three hours sleep in the afternoon. He went to his GP who took a series of blood tests. John went onto herbal remedies when he saw a programme on TV on chronic fatigue. John's uncle is a physician in genetics and he set him up with an English specialist consultant. He felt the ensuing assessment was a waste of time as it told him what he knew. He then went to Liverpool for further blood tests. He saw a local specialist in 1994 who took blood tests and suspected his gut permeability.

John has tried alternative medicine via acupuncture. He is extremely fussy about his food and when he takes sugar he suffers from nose bleeds and headaches. When he takes wheat his temperature rises and he cannot sleep. These are immediate responses. After dairy products his joints seize up. After nuts and seeds he suffers diarrhoea. Wheat also gives him diarrhoea.

Several of the local specialists were suggesting that John's difficulties were psychological, and so in the summer of 1994 he came to see me.

Presenting symptoms
John, at interview, presented the following symptoms:

- He constantly feels tired and fatigued.
- He doesn't recover from exercise fast enough, and certainly not before the next exercise session.
- His sleeping patterns are irregular.
- He reports a series of sore throats.

- During a race he starts well but after a few laps feels he has no power, it hurts and he just loses everything.
- Sometimes he feels completely exhausted, even after 12 hours' sleep and a sleep during the day.
- He suffers from food allergies with nose bleeds and headaches after sugar, high temperature and sleeplessness after wheat.
- His joints "seize up" after dairy products.
- Nuts, seeds and wheat give him diarrhoea.

A haematology and biochemistry analysis from Diagnostic Services Ltd was carried out. Dr Edwards (in November 1993) reported haematology leucocytes 2.4 (normal range 4-11); neutrophils 59 per cent, 1.42, (normal range 2-7.5); lymphocytes at 36 per cent, 0.86 (normal range 1.5-4); and Platelets 108 (normal range 150-400). The subject's white blood cells show leucopenia with neutrophils and lymphocytes reduced. Platelets are reduced. Cholesterol 3.2, normal range 3.6-6. All other blood measures, i.e. haemoglobin, erythrocytes, glucose, urea, creatinine, phosphate, triglycerides, bilirubin, protein, albumin, globulin are within the normal range. Anaemia is not indicated. John's scores on the Eysenck Personality Scales (1991) are given in Table 1.

Table 1. Eysenck Personality Scales EPQ–R and IVE: John's scores

	Norm $\bar{x}$	
Tender Minded	7 λ 10	Tough (Psychotic) Minded
Introvert	λ 5 13	Extravert
Stable	12 λ 18	Emotional – Neurotic
Low Impulsiveness	λ 1 7	Impulsive
Low Venturesome	7 λ 12	Venturesome
Low Empathy	13 λ 14	Empathy
Low Addiction	12 λ 17	Addiction
Low Social Desirability	λ 4 7	Social Desirability – Lie Scale

Assessment

John is, according to the Eysenck Personality Scales, a "neurotic-introvert". He is on the tough-minded side of the psychotic dimension. He is low in impulsiveness, but prepared to venture once he knows what risks are involved. His score for empathy is normal. What is most interesting is his score for addiction, which is five points above the norm. Social desirability is low, suggesting that he has answered this questionnaire in an honest and open fashion. Eysenck Personality Scales are particularly useful for assessing personality traits and types within sport, as they clearly indicate preferences for tough-minded/tender-mindedness, extrovert-introvert, stable-neurotic, risk taking and the likelihood of showing addictive behaviour. In the sense that John's score for addiction is high, this would indicate that his personality would lead him towards exercise addiction, other things being equal. Eysenck et al. (1982) point out the importance of inspecting trait aspects of personality and here is an example of the importance of such measurement in order to obtain some prediction towards addictive behaviour. Studies in the past using Eysenck's Personality Scales have concentrated on the extroversion-introversion dimension.

Therapy

A cognitive behaviour approach was taken with John which looked at his whole life. It was quite clear that food and mood were related in his system, and the following two cycles (Figures 1 and 2) were discussed with a view to his rejecting the old circle of life and adopting the new one.

Next I suggested John change his daily schedule (Figure 3). The next cognitive behavioural technique for therapy involved hypnosis (see Figure 4).

Cripps et al. (1994), in their review of the applications of hypnosis in sport and exercise settings, report generally positive effects on mood. Certainly a reduction of negative mood states has been empirically demonstrated (Norell et al., 1994). A self-hypnosis session was recorded on tape according to the following protocol:

Induction: induction involved relaxation and then paying attention to single stimuli, one at a time. The first of these were the sounds outside of the room; next, sounds inside the room; and thirdly, paying attention to the position of various body parts, finishing with the head. The emphasis in the induction was on relaxation and positive feelings of wellbeing. The induction continued with focusing on the join between the eyelids and relaxation in the hands and fingers.

Deepening: the deepening exercise involves counting down from nine in three's, to deep exhalations of breath. This simulates going down through three levels of deeper relaxation, encouraging the subject to relax more and more deeply.

Special place: the special place technique reported by Callow in Cripps et al. (1994) was used twice on two separate sound tapes. Tape 1 was for relaxation. Tape 2 was for recovery, and in John's case, this was during a race,and was a very active special place indeed. During this special place of John's, he could see a downhill stretch of mountain biking countryside, hear the crowd and all the cheering going on and feel that it wanted him to go harder, take risks, do it for the crowd, and, in his own words, "burn into the floor".

Auto suggestions: there followed a series of auto suggestions which we discussed. These were to do with feeling good, organized, clean, satisfied, relaxed, healthy and fit, looking to the future, and above all, feeling better. The auto suggestions were

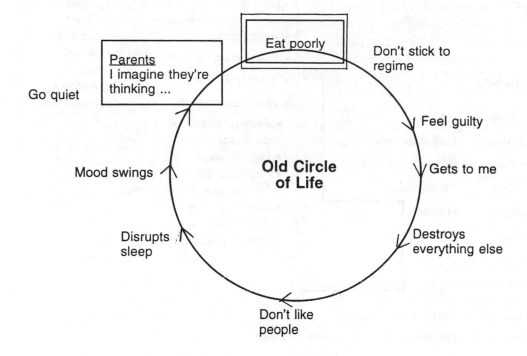

Figure 1. Old circle of life – addiction

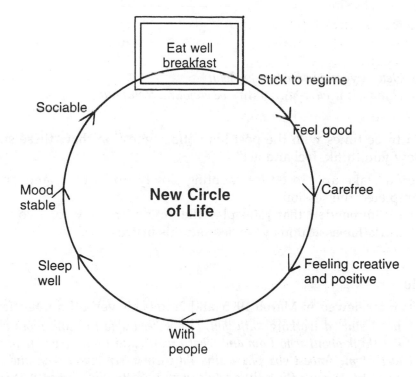

Figure 2. New circle of life – commitment

Figure 3

Figure 4

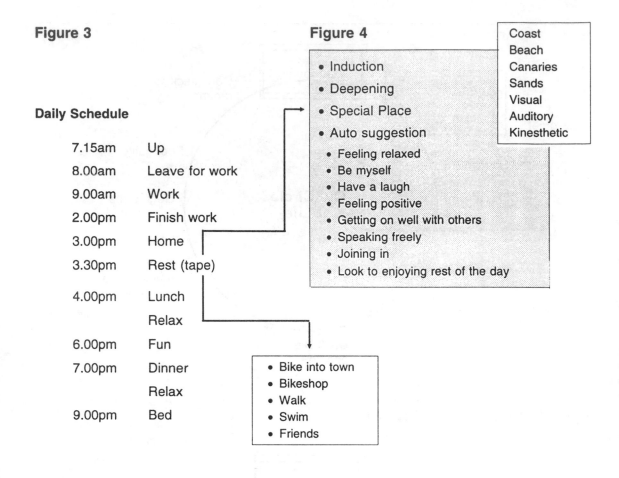

Figure 3: New suggested schedule for John
Figure 4: Hypnosis used as a cognitive behavioural technique

repeated three times with the post hypnotic suggestion that "these suggestions will affect how you think, feel and act".

Wake-up: a wake-up procedure counting slowly up to nine, and opening eyes on nine, completed the session.

I recommended that John play the tape every day for two weeks when he finished work. He assiduously carried out this instruction.

Results

John was interviewed in March 1995, and here is his verbatim interview:

> *Since I started working with you, I have been able to think more clearly about my life. I think about who I am and what I want, and I am now able to focus on myself. I was at my lowest ebb physically. I'd been to see everybody, and although things seemed to improve for a little while, nothing actually worked. I am now more positive, more determined and am back on track towards recovery.*

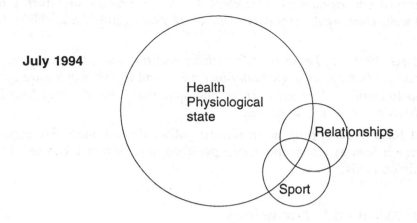

Figure 5. Integrated life approach – life plan out of balance

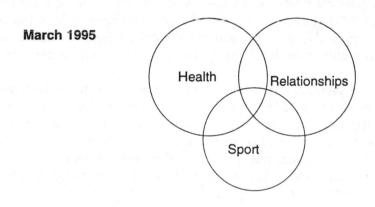

Figure 6. Life plan more in balance

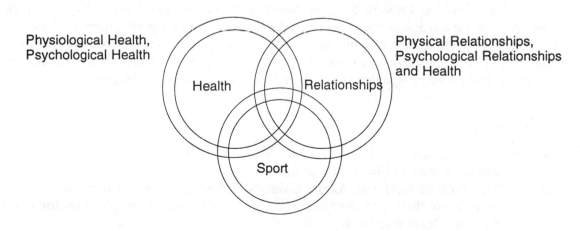

Figure 7. The future integrated life plan to include a psychological dimension

I actually played my self-hypnosis tape every day for four weeks, and during those weeks I felt well, knew what I was doing and where I was going. I was able to think realistically.

Now, in March 1995, my health is better, I have realistic goals, I can plan my life more effectively. My training is gradually increasing and my level of leisure cycling is nearly up to training. I go out running and swimming. For the first time I am beginning to think like a normal person.

I surprised John by dropping in on him to gather these results. He certainly appeared to be much less anxious and more positive, and when I chatted to his parents, they confirmed this.

Prognosis, discussion and conclusions

This intervention has taken an Integrated Life Approach. This is to say I have looked at three aspects of John's life: first, his own physical health and physiological functioning; secondly his sport; and thirdly his relationships with others. If we are to represent each of these three areas by interlinking circles, they would look like Figure 5. John has now managed to adjust his life plan into a more balanced lifestyle, where his health, relationships and sport are on a more even level (see Figure 6). John no longer reports any form of fatigue.

This is only half the picture, and to stop here would be completely neglecting the psychological dimension. What was previously missing in John's life was an understanding of the importance of psychological wellbeing. Now that a psychological perspective has been introduced, his integrated life plan looks very different. John now has a psychological dimension for his health, relationships and sport, which is in fact more dominant and subsumes the physical. Eventually, of course, the psychological and physical should merge to give equal input into those vital areas of John's life (Figure 7).

By adopting a cognitive behavioural approach and using the powerful conditioning of words in post-hypnotic suggestion, John is well on the way to recovery.

He is looking forward to competition again, but it is still very early along the way. A way forward will be to begin a Mental Skills Training Programme. This will introduce a psychological dimension into John's mountain biking in order to increase control of psychological mechanisms and condition them to be able to handle a training and competitive programme leading on to success and out of decline.

References

Bakker, F.C., Whiting, H.T.A. and Van der Brug, H. (1990). *Sport psychology: Concepts and applications.* John Wiley & Sons.

Cripps, B.D., Callow, G., Pope, A. and Cann, G. (1994). *Hypnosis in sport and exercise: A review of theory, research and practice.* Paper presented to BPS London Conference, December 1994.

Eysenck, H.J. and Eysenck, S.B.G. (1991). *Adult EPQ-R, Adult IVE.* Hodder and Stoughton.

Eysenck, H.J, Nias, D.K.B. and Cox, D.N. (1982). Sport and personality. *Advances in Behaviour Research and Therapy, 4,* 1-15.

Glasser, W. (1976). *Positive Addiction.* New York: Harper & Row.

Pargman, D. and Burgess, S. (1979). Hooked on exercise: A Psycho-biological explanation; motor skills: *Theory into Practice, 3,* 2, 115-122.

Steinberg, H. and Sykes, E.A. (1985). Introduction to symposium on endorphins and behavioural processes; Review of literature on endorphins and exercise. *Pharmacology, Biochemistry and Behaviour, 23,* 857-862.

Steinberg, H., Sykes, E.A. and Morris, M. (1990). Exercise addiction: The opiate connection. Sport, health psychology and exercise symposium. London, Sports Council, pp.161-166.

Veale, D.M.W. (1987a). Exercise addiction. *British Journal of Addiction, 82,* 735-740.

Veale, D.M.W. (1987b). Exercise and mental health. *Acta Psychiatrica Scandinavica, 76,* 113-120.

Whiting, H.T.A. (1994). *Exercise addiction: motivation for participation in sport and exercise.* Submission for a Satellite Professional Development Workshop, The British Psychological Society, Sport and Exercise Psychology Section.

5

Exercise Addiction, Mood and Body Image: A Complex Inter-relationship

D.F. Sewell, P.J. Clough and L. Robertshaw

Baekland (1970) first proposed that exercisers can become addicted to exercise after noting the difficulty he had in recruiting volunteers for a study which required regular exercisers to abstain from exercise. Glasser (1975) populariz'ed the idea that it was possible to become addicted to exercise, suggesting that exercise produces a positive addiction. This view has become less popular and the concept of negative addiction, first suggested by Morgan (1979), has become the dominant conceptual framework.

Most of the research into exercise addiction has used samples of runners, and the findings reported suggest that addicted runners suffer withdrawal symptoms when they are unable to run (e.g. Morgan, 1979; Peele, 1979; Sachs and Pargman, 1979). This narrow focus on runners may have led researchers to conclude prematurely that the research question is now "how does addiction come about?" rather than fully investigating whether or not exercise addiction actually exists. Whilst the previous research suggests that when regular runners are prevented from running their mood states deteriorate, the literature is almost silent in relation to addiction to other aerobic sports and has paid little attention to the possibility of addiction in non-aerobic activities.

Body image has been found to be a major factor in exercise involvement (e.g. Clough et al., 1989) and it has been suggested that it may have a major role to play in the genesis and maintenance of exercise addiction. For example, Chan and Grossman (1988) have demonstrated that withdrawal from running can result in a distorted body image.

To broaden and further investigate exercise addiction we compared two groups of exercisers, regular runners and regular golfers. This comparison had three main aims: (a) to compare the degree of commitment/addiction to the two activities; (b) to relate an involvement in both activities to mood states; and (c) to examine the relationship between body image and participation.

Method

Subjects

Forty four individuals (male n=34, female n=10) participated in this study. Twenty two were runners and 22 were golfers. The runners' sample consisted of 15 males and seven females. Their ages ranged from 21 to 65 (mean=42.3, sd=8.64). Running experience ranged from one to 50 years (mean=10.4, sd=10.3). Their weekly mileage averaged 24.5 miles (sd=12.3). The golfers sample was made up of three females and 19 males. Their mean age was 44.5 (sd=9.1) and their golfing experience ranged from three to 30 years (mean 14.5 years; sd=8.6). The mean participation rate was 1.6 times per week (sd=0.6).

Measures

Body image

The assessment of body image was carried out using four different approaches. Subjects were presented with two nine-figure silhouette scales, one for each sex, based on those developed by Stunkard et al. (1983). Subjects were asked to select the silhouette which corresponded to their current figure and also to their ideal figure. In addition they rated different parts of their body using a five-point scale and completed a global rating of their weight. Finally, subjects' actual body make-up was assessed by comparing their weight and height with the Body Mass Index (BMI) chart.

Commitment/addiction

A bespoke questionnaire was developed as a direct measure of addiction. This 14-item scale, which employed a five-point rating system, measured both negative addiction and positive addiction and was based on the commitment to running scale developed by Carmack and Martens (1979) and on Hailey and Bailey's (1982) negative addiction scale. The wording was modified for golfers where necessary. Positive feelings about participation were measured by six items (e.g. running/golfing is pleasant, running/golfing is the high point of my life). Negative addiction was measured in two ways. Negative feelings associated with non-participation were measured by two items (e.g. on days that I do not play golf/do not run, I feel depressed or mentally sluggish) and negative feelings towards participation were measured by six items (e.g. I wish there was a more enjoyable way to stay fit; I dread the thought of running/golfing).

Mood measures

The mood measures provided an indirect measure of addiction. The relationship between participation in either golf or running and participants' mood states was determined using a daily mood diary. This method was adopted as it is very sensitive to variations in mood states. Subjects were asked to rate their moods for 28 days using six bipolar scales: relaxed-tense; energetic-weary; depressed-elated; tired-alert; anxious-calm; and cheerful-miserable. If the participants ran or played golf, they rated their moods "just before" and "just after" participation. Subjects also recorded their exercise involvement on each of the 28 days.

Design and procedure

A four-week daily mood diary was distributed to all respondents during the months of February and March. A body image questionnaire was posted to each subject weekly. The commitment/addiction questionnaire was sent out in the final week of the study.

Results

Both golfers and runners were positive about their sport (runners mean=3.47, sd=3.6; golfers mean=3.5, sd=7.5) but the golfers were significantly more negative (t=2.04, p<0.05) about their involvement (mean=3.4, sd=0.4) than the runners (mean=1.4, sd=0.5).

The assessment of mood states revealed a number of differences between the runners and golfers. Over the 28-day period of the study golfers were more cheerful, elated, energetic, alert, calm and relaxed. These results are shown in Table 1.

Table 1. Differences in average mood states (measured over 28 days) between golfers and runners

Mood states	Runners Mean	sd	Golfers Mean	sd	t-value
Relaxed	32.9	5.8	36.5	5.1	2.2
Energetic	27.3	5.8	29.3	6.3	1.1
Elated	25.8	4.6	27.5	5.0	1.1
Alert	22.6	6.5	24.5	8.1	0.9
Calm	27.8	7.2	31.2	6.3	1.6
Cheerful	32.1	6.7	34.5	7.0	1.2

The higher the mean score the more positive the mood state.
*p<0.05

The direct impact of participation was assessed by comparing the subjects' mood states just before taking part and just after. These results are shown in Table 2.

Table 2. Comparison of the impact of golfing and running on mood states

Mood states	Runners mean	sd	Golfers mean	sd	t-value
Relaxed	+7.5	7.5	+4.2	8.1	1.4
Energetic	+3.2	8.4	+0.6	11.3	0.8
Elated	+4.5	7.1	-6.1	10.2	4.0**
Alert	+0.8	11.3	-11.3	10.3	3.5**
Calm	+1.4	7.9	-6.7	10.5	2.9*
Cheerful	+7.1	4.6	+4.6	8.2	1.2

** p<0.01; *p<0.05

Participation in running appears to bring greater benefits to runners than golfing brings to golfers. In fact, participation in golfing leads to a more depressed state and greater levels of fatigue and anxiety.

The final analysis investigating mood states and exercise participation was a comparison of the days golfers played golf and the days they did not and the days runners did not run and the days on which they participated.

Table 3. Comparison of mean mood states on participation days (before and after the activity) and non-participation days for golfers and runners

Golfers	Relaxed	Energy	Elated	Alert	Calm	Cheerful
Before	33.3	36.6	30.8	36.5	38.3	32.0
After	37.5	37.2	24.7	24.8	31.7	36.6
No activity	31.6	34.3	24.1	32.1	29.7	31.2
Runners						
Before	25.4	23.1	21.4	24.0	29.8	25.8
After	32.9	26.3	25.6	28.1	31.2	32.9
No activity	24.8	32.3	18.2	25.4	27.2	23.2

The comparison of mood states on participation and non-participation days produces a complex picture. For the golfers it appears that their mood states are generally at their most positive just before they start a round of golf. Overall their moods after golfing, although worse than just before, are more positive than on non-golfing days. Runners appear to be at their most positive directly after running. Few differences exist between "no-run days" mood states and mood states measured directly prior to going on a run.

It was found that the runners were less accurate in their perceptions of their weight. Forty five per cent of the runners rated themselves as overweight although their BMI scores suggested that they fell into the normal range, whereas 27 per cent of the golfers similarly overestimated their weight status. Similarly, runners were significantly more dissatisfied with their bodies (t=1.68, p<0.05) and reported a higher discrepancy between their present self and their ideal self (t=1.65, p<0.05).

Discussion

The present research was designed as a pilot for a far more extensive investigation of addiction in aerobic exercise, non-aerobic exercise and non-exercise based leisure activities. The small number of participants, and the high levels of variability within the two samples, means that the findings reported must be treated with a degree of caution.

Both runners and golfers appear to be committed to their activity. Commitment in this paper refers to positive feelings about their chosen activity. Both samples were, perhaps not surprisingly, very positive about their chosen activities. In addition, both samples showed some evidence of negative addiction. This was measured by subjects rating the consequences of non-participation. The existence of apparent addiction in a non-aerobic activity is felt to be particularly important. Investigations into exercise addiction have concentrated on aerobic activities, especially running. This narrow focus may have led researchers to place too much emphasis on possible biochemical explanations of exercise addiction, as these appear to offer a plausible mechanism with which to explain the research findings. However, if further research can replicate the findings reported here, that non-aerobic activities can produce signs of positive and negative addiction, the emphasis of research may need to change. It is suggested here that exercise addiction is far from a proven entity. Exercise addiction may be simply a sub-set of commitment and/or addiction to a wide range of human work and leisure based activities. If this is the case the recent emphasis on biochemical explanations of exercise addiction may have to be re-evaluated.

One difference between the golfers and runners, in relation to the data derived from the commitment/addiction questionnaire, was that golfers were significantly more negative about their activity than were runners, although as previously stated they were equally positive about their activity. In other words the "pull" that running and golfing have on their respective participants is roughly equal, but in golf there is also a barrier that may act to prevent or reduce participation.

One possible explanation of this apparent anomaly may lie in the differences observed in the impact on psychological wellbeing of participation in the two activities. In general, runners appear to receive a high degree of psychological enhancement as a result of their running. This supports previous research (e.g. Peele, 1978). Participation in running often produces a "post-run high". The situation for golfers is quite different. Golfers appear to experience a pre-golf high, in other words mood enhancement is greatest just before starting a round. This high appears to vanish during the golf round, with golfers becoming less elated, less alert and less calm after they finish. This pattern of mood variations may be explained by the nature of the game of golf. Performance is very quantifiable and even slight variations in the quality of an individual's play can have a major impact on scores. This may lead to frustration and lower mood as the final result does not meet the high expectations prior to the game.

Up to this point we have discussed the findings relating to the direct measures of addiction. The present study also allows a more indirect approach to be used; a comparison of mood on the days people exercise with the days they did not take part. Again a different pattern emerges for runners and golfers. Overall, runners' mood states appear to be very similar on "non-run" days and just before they run. However, runners' mood states are significantly more positive after running than either before the run or on non-run days. Golfers' moods on non-golf days appear to be similar to their post-golf mood states but overall both of these are lower than the pre-golf measures. This raises an important methodological point. It is possible to argue from the findings reported here that both golfers and runners suffer mood declines when they do not take part in their activities, suggesting some degree of addiction. However, the conclusions that can be drawn are dependent on when the measures are taken. Running appears to boost mood, but non-running may not cause a decline in mood, rather it may simply mean that the runners do not get the apparently "short term buzz" associated with participation. Comparing post-run measures with non-run day measures may indeed reveal a difference, but it may also be seen as setting up a "straw man" argument, suggesting a "cold turkey" phenomenon that may not exist. Golfers present a different measurement problem. If you compare non-golf days with post-golf measures there appear to be few mood differences, but a comparison of pre-golf measures with non-golf day measures may indeed suggest deprivation effects.

The importance of body image in the addiction process receives some support from the present study. Runners were more negative about their body image than the golfers, despite the fact that the objective measures of body image, the BMI measures, did not differ between the two groups. The motivational impact of body image has been demonstrated in a number of previous studies (e.g. Clough et al., 1989). The distortion of body image reported here may present runners with a problem. Exercising to improve one's body image when the exerciser is overestimating his or her weight problems may lead to ultimate dissatisfaction as they will find it difficult to reduce their weight further, and this could conceivably lead to exercise abuse or dietary deficiencies.

References

Backland, F. (1970). Exercise deprivation: sleep and psychological reactions. *Archives of General Psychiatry*, 22, 365-369.

Carmack, M.A. and Martens, R. (1979). Measuring commitment to running: A survey of runners' attitudes and mental states. *Journal of Sport Behaviour*, 5, 150-154.

Chan, C.S. and Grossman, H.Y. (1988). Psychological effects of running loss on consistent runners. *Perceptual and Motor Skills*, 66, 875-883.

Clough, P.J., Shepherd, J. and Maughan, R.J. (1989). Motives for participation in recreational running. *Journal of Leisure Research*, 21, 297-309.

Glasser, W. (1975.) *Positive addiction*. New York: Harper & Row.

Morgan, W.P. (1979). Negative addiction in runners. *The Physician and Sports Medicine*, 7, 57-70.

Peele, S. (1981). How much is too much? *Healthier habits or destructive addictions*. New York: Prentice Hall.

Sachs, M.L. and Pargman, D. (1979). Running addiction: A depth interview examination. *Journal of Sport Psychology*, 2, 143-155.

Stunkard, A.J., Sorenson, T. and Schulsinger, F. (1983). Use of the Danish adoption register for the study of obesity and thinness. In S. Kety (Ed.) *The genetics of neurological and psychiatric disorders*. New York: Raven (pp.115-120).

6

Hooked on the 'Buzz': History of a Body-Building Addict

Carole Seheult

This case study comprises the referral, assessment and formulation of the psychological difficulties experienced by a 36-year-old male body-builder who sought help for a problem which he perceived to be an addiction to the "adrenaline buzz" associated with carrying out an intensive regime of weight lifting which formed part of preparation for competitive body-building. The report also makes recommendations as to possible courses of action which might alleviate his particular problems and poses questions regarding the referral, assessment and treatment of people suffering from addictive behaviour of this kind.

Referral

Mr E is a 36-year-old self-confessed body-building addict about whom I was originally consulted in June 1994. At that time, Mr E, who lives in the north-west of England, had been referred by his GP to a local physiotherapist interested in sports medicine, with the hope that the physiotherapist would be able to help Mr E by suggesting some alternative form of exercise and thus wean him away from the activity to which he had become addicted. On meeting Mr E however, the physiotherapist was concerned to find that his obsession with body-building had become very resistant to change and also that Mr E's mood seemed significantly depressed. Recognizing a need for a more in-depth evaluation of his patient's difficulties, the physiotherapist came to the decision that referral to a psychologist might be the answer.

At first this recommendation was readily accepted both by the GP and by Mr E himself. However, despite his initial enthusiasm, Mr E subsequently decided he would try to change his behaviour on his own and a formal referral did not materialize. Five months later, in November 1994, I was again approached regarding Mr E, this time with a formal referral letter from his GP in which his current difficulties were described.

Background history

In his letter the GP described Mr E as an "obsessive fitness fanatic" with a 15-year history of "diligent adherence" to body-building and diet and as deriving a "high" from the physical fitness which he constantly maintained.

In the summer of 1994 Mr E had consulted his doctor saying that he wanted to wind down his body-building activities but was finding that as a result of withdrawal from the regime he was feeling psychologically quite low. Although, in the GP's opinion, Mr E was not, at that time, clinically depressed, when he saw him a month later he felt that Mr E's mood had deteriorated and subsequently, in August 1994, prescribed Clomipramine which his patient was continuing to find helpful.

By November 1994 Mr E was still not feeling much better about his lifestyle and the dominating role played in it by body-building, and, as a result, contacted his GP, this time requesting a referral to see a sports psychologist. An appointment was subsequently arranged.

Interview and assessment

On meeting, Mr E presented as a pleasant but slightly reserved person who was nevertheless quite happy to discuss with me what he saw as being his difficulties.

He began by describing what he perceived to be a very "normal" life despite the problems related to the body-building. He was in full time employment as a postman, was reasonably satisfied with his job and had no particular aspirations to develop his career in any different direction. At that time Mr E was living at home with his parents and described his relationship with them as "good".

Mr E described his physical health as "excellent", although he said that he was still continuing to take Clomipramine for his depressed mood. In 1991 he had suffered from a bout of severe depression and had been hospitalized for four weeks in a local psychiatric hospital. Following this episode Mr E had got married but this had only lasted for four weeks and had ended under very acrimonious circumstances. There were no children.

Mr E told me that he had first became involved in body-building approximately 11 years previously and since that time had developed a good enough physique to enter a number of regional level competitions. Prior to a competition, over an extended period of several weeks, Mr E followed a strict dietary regime coupled with intensive strength and weight training in the gym. During pre-competition periods he would go to the gym seven days a week for two-hour sessions using static Nautilus type weight and strength training machines. This training had therefore come to dominate his entire way of life and took up most of his free time.

As well as the weight training, a further aspect of Mr E's competition preparation was the dietary regime which he adopted. In general, this diet consisted of a rather limited range of food – pasta, rice and tuna fish. Talking to Mr E it seemed that the imposition of this very stringent dieting had created for him a somewhat distorted attitude toward food which at certain times he had come only to see as "fuel" for the moulding of his body into the desired form. Although describing himself as "fed up" with eating pasta, tuna and rice, he did not seem to have any real idea of what he would prefer to eat. He did his own cooking.

When asked specifically, Mr E told me that he was a "natural" body-builder and had never taken any illegal substances to improve his physique. He said that he had at times taken Primasorb, a substance which is said to enable better absorption of food and which Mr E also told me gave him an "incredible high". As far as he saw it, the weight and strength training developed muscle bulk and the restricted high protein diet reduced fat levels thus providing the much desired muscle definition for which competitive body-builders all strive.

Current problems

At the time of our meeting, Mr E described his main problem as his dilemma regarding continuing with the weight training and body-building. He said he did not want to enter further competitions, but reducing the level of training could bring about a number of negative consequences. One problem was that without what he perceived to be a "moderate" amount of weight training he would feel himself to be deteriorating physically and he was frightened that, knowing he was no longer feeling or looking as good as he wished, he would become even more depressed. This perception of physical deterioration and loss of physique were, in his opinion, what made him depressed and he was extremely fearful that withdrawal effects might precipitate a further bout of severe depression entailing psychiatric intervention.

With regard to his current feelings of depression, he said that these had eased slightly, but this improvement seemed entirely related to the medication rather than any resolution of the dilemma which he saw as being the main cause of his problems. He regretted that in the past he had not had the opportunity for counselling or psychotherapy.

A further difficulty for Mr E was the potential loss of the intermittent, but highly rewarding, "buzz" or "high" attributed by him to the adrenaline generated by intensive exercise. If he was to give up the training this would no longer be achievable and it was this that he seemed neither able nor willing to accept. He said that over the years he had become "hooked" on the "buzz" which he experienced on a regular but somewhat unpredictable basis when engaged in using the weight machines. He found this phenomenon very pleasant and it would appear likely that this had become a major reinforcer for continuing to exercise at a consistently high level. At various times when he had decreased the intensity of training, he had found himself no longer able to achieve the "buzz", thus he had come to the conclusion that there was a minimal level of training which he had to maintain in order to receive this positive reinforcer.

For him, the resultant dilemma was that if he continued to exercise at the necessary level to produce the adrenaline "buzz", his lifestyle would continue to be dominated by the body-building regime and going to the gym several times a week. On the other hand, if he stopped the regime, he would no longer achieve the rewarding rush of adrenaline and would also lose his feeling of fitness and being in good shape which he had convinced himself was necessary for his psychological wellbeing.

As well as his interest and involvement in physical exercise a number of other areas of Mr E's current and past life were explored. In particular there was considerable discussion of the history surrounding his relationship with his former wife. This included his "nervous breakdown" and the period of hospitalization for depression which had resulted; his marriage and its subsequent breakdown after only four weeks; his wife's alleged physical violence towards him and a court appearance as a result of her pressing charges against him for violent behaviour. After talking to Mr E, it appeared that there were still a number of issues resulting from this period of his life which were still far from being resolved. Despite the admitted acrimony surrounding these events he still felt it would be completely impossible to find anyone else with whom he could form such a close relationship.

Formulation

From a theoretical point of view it would seem fairly clear that Mr E falls into the category of an "addicted" athlete conforming to the definition put forward by Heil (1994) who defines the syndrome in behavioural terms as "the need to perform a given activity regularly to maintain emotional equilibrium". Heil goes on to describe the negatively addicted athlete as someone who continues to train intensively despite adverse effects upon other aspects of life, for example, work or interpersonal relationships (Morgan, 1979). He describes the key feature of this type of behaviour as being not so much the volume of training that is undertaken but more the compulsive style with which it is pursued, despite the negative consequences. Withdrawal symptoms are said to include depression, anxiety, irritability, interpersonal difficulties and a number of somatic disturbances including problems with sleep (Heil, 1994). All of these symptoms had been experienced by Mr E.

In terms of the underlying psychological factors thought to be operating, that of low self-esteem has generally been seen as one of the major factors (Hays, 1990). For a large period of Mr E's life success in competitive body building, as well as the more specifically pleasurable effects achieved when training, have played a dominant role in how he spends his time. The difficult and traumatic relationship with his former wife and the emotional sequel of their separation seem to have provided a severe blow to his self-esteem. However, by the very nature of his personality, Mr E finds great difficulty in looking at these issues and when seen in November 1994, despite the intervening period of almost four years, many were far from resolved. This "stickiness" and unwillingness to look at change are probably symptomatic of fairly entrenched beliefs and attitudes inherent in Mr E"s personality. The therapeutic task in this situation might therefore have a lot to do with his willingness to explore alternatives and options especially in lifestyle.

Conclusions

Overall, my feeling after seeing Mr E was that it would probably be of no advantage for him to continue to see me for help with his problems as the type of therapy or counselling which I felt he needed was likely to be just as readily and appropriately available from the clinical psychologists within his own area. Also, I did not feel that it was his involvement in sport or physical activity that was the only reason for his difficulties, although, over the years, it would seem that the training programme and dietary regime had become their major focus.

This case study highlights a number of issues related to the area of exercise addiction and also prompts a number of questions about who is the most appropriate person to see people with this type of problem? What kinds of assessment are most likely to provide understanding and finally what kind of therapeutic approach is most likely to benefit the client?

References

Heil, J. (1993). Specialised treatment approaches: Problems in rehabilitation. In J. Heil (Ed.) Psychology of sport injury. *Human Kinetics, Ill.*

Morgan, W.P. (1979). Negative addiction in runners. *The Physician and Sports Medicine, 7, 2, 57-63/67-69.*

Hays, K.F. (1990). *Negative addiction: When bad things happen to good sports.* Paper presented at the meeting of the Association for the Advancement of Applied Sport Psychology, San Antonio, TX, September 1990.

7

A Cognitive-Behavioural Approach to Excessive Exercise

Konstantinos S. Loumidis & Hillary Roxborough

There has been increasing interest in Excessive Exercising (EE) following recognition of this as a clinical condition which entails some physical and psychological risk. At the moment, consensus concerning the theoretical framework, definitional criteria and clinical features of EE, has not been established. One of the reasons for this is the lack of established measures to diagnose and assess this disorder. The lack of understanding of the aetiological and maintaining factors of the condition has important implications in clinical practice.

Definitions

A variety of definitions has been proposed to describe the condition. These tend to fall into three categories: those which emphasize the compulsive nature of the behaviour (e.g., morbid exercising: Chalmers et al., 1985; obligatory running: Blumenthal et al., 1984; obligatory exercising: Passman and Thompson, 1988), those emphasizing a relationship between excessive exercise and anorexia (e.g., analogue to anorexia: Yates, 1983; running anorexia: Noval, 1980; activity based anorexia: Epling et al., 1983) and those that classify it as an addiction (e.g., negative addiction: Morgan, 1979; positive addiction: Glasser, 1976; running addiction: Sachs, 1981).

Until the aetiology of EE is better understood, we recommend the use of a broader definition of excessive exercising (EE), that is, engagement in exercise which is carried out to an excessive degree and which is associated with psychological and physical risk. It is suggested that this has the following advantages: first, it is a generic term which focuses on the behaviour of excessive exercising rather than making any specific claims concerning the aetiology of the condition; secondly, excessive exercising is shared in all aetiological models while other terms (such as compulsion, anorexia) may not; thirdly, at a clinical level it can provide an objective measure (or symptom) of the condition.

Theoretical models of excessive exercising

A variety of theoretical models of excessive exercising has been proposed. In this section each of these will be critically evaluated and a cognitive behavioural model will then be proposed.

(a) Excessive exercising and eating disorders

There has been considerable interest in the proposed relationship between excessive exercising and eating disorders. Eisler and LeGrange (1990) have described the following possible types of relationship: (1) anorexia nervosa (AN) and excessive exercise (EE) form distinct diagnostic groups; (2) AN and EE are overlapping groups and EE can lead to the development of AN; (3) AN and EE are both related to some other common underlying disorder; and (4) EE is a variant of eating disorder. Each has been supported on theoretical as well as empirical grounds.

However, Eisler and LeGrange acknowledged the fact that first, these models are not mutually exclusive, secondly, that "different models apply to different individuals or different groups of individuals" and thirdly, "most of the available data do little to distinguish between the suggested models" (p.382). They also criticized the methodology as being based on anecdotal case reports or very small numbers of subjects.

It appears that the relationship between EE and AN may be theoretically and clinically significant, although the nature of this relationship needs to be established. It is proposed that investigating similarities and differences in underlying beliefs and attitudes, and information processing biases relating to body image and food, will help to clarify the relationship between EE and AN and distinguish between these models.

(b) Excessive exercise as a physiological addiction

Physiological models of addiction to exercise have emphasized the role of endorphins or cortisol in the maintenance of excessive exercising. Morris et al. (1990) deprived a group of regular runners from exercising and concluded that their findings were consistent with the view that exercise increases endorphin activity, producing an addiction and resulting in a withdrawal syndrome if stopped. Although there is other evidence to support this (e.g., with dogs: Radovich et al., 1989) one study has found that scores on exercise dependence are not related to changes in plasma beta-endorphin levels after aerobic exercise (Pierce et al., 1993). It is also generally accepted that positive changes in mood after exercise are more associated with moderate, rather than high, levels of exercise intensity (Steptoe and Bolton, 1988; Steptoe and Cox, 1988). Therefore the evidence is currently inconclusive. It can also be argued that there is an element of circularity in these models where cause and effect are difficult to disentangle.

Therefore the extent of the role of physiological addiction in excessive exercising is at an early stage of understanding in terms of theoretical validity and clinical utility. However if this does prove to be a significant aetiological factor in EE, recent developments in cognitive models of different disorders emphasize the importance of defining the mediating role of cognition in addictive behaviour. Therefore, a gap in current physiological models is the lack of understanding of the underlying cognitions which are associated with excessive exercising as a physiological addiction.

(c) Personality factors in excessive exercising

It has been proposed that excessive exercising can be explained in terms of personality traits or characteristics.

46

Yates et al. (1983) reported that high self-imposed expectations, a tendency towards depression and exercise denial, were personality traits shared between excessive exercisers and anorexics. Sacks (1987) argued that although EE and anorexia may exist independently, they both share a central narcissistic dynamic driven by either the pursuit of physical effectiveness (in excessive exercisers) or the pursuit of physical attractiveness (in anorexics). Pierce et al. (1993) argued that the high incidence of EE and AN among dancers could be attributed to a need to achieve high technical proficiency (EE) and a predetermined ideal body composition (AN).

In contrast, Blumenthal et al. (1984) demonstrated that obligatory runners score significantly lower psychopathological MMPI scores when compared with patients with AN. It appears that there may be certain personality variables which are characteristic of EE, but the evidence suggests that these may not always be sufficiently severe to warrant a label of psychopathology according to certain criteria. However, identifying specific personality characteristics is important as this enables a fuller understanding of the development of cognitive biases and distortions and subsequent behaviour according to the cognitive model of different disorders.

A proposed cognitive-behavioural model of excessive exercising

The review of existing theoretical models has indicated an important gap in the current understanding of the mediating cognitive factors in EE, namely underlying beliefs, dysfunctional thoughts and biases in information processing. This section will propose a cognitive-behavioural model which attempts to fill this gap.

There have been a variety of cognitive-behavioural models proposed to describe the development and maintenance of various disorders (e.g., obsessive compulsive disorder: Salkovskis, 1985; panic disorder: Clark, 1986, eating disorders: Slade, 1982; depression: Beck, 1967, 1976; hypochondriasis: Salkovskis and Warwick, 1986). These models share the same essential cognitive structures (i.e., schemata, automatic thoughts) and processes (i.e., errors in thinking) although the content of these differs for different disorders. It is proposed that the same basic cognitive-behavioural model can be adapted to account for the aetiology and maintenance of excessive exercising. This is presented in Table 1.

A number of exercisers may use exercise as an intuitively positive means to manage stress. However, a thorough and deeper level functional analysis may reveal negative views about one's self (i.e., I am unattractive, I am unwanted) or a pathological personality profile (i.e., dependent, narcissistic, addictive). The cognitive model proposes that personality styles form the superordinate schemata or most basic and deeply held beliefs about the self. These influence the development of the schemata or rules that individuals hold about themselves and the world. In EE these could be shared with anorexics ("To be wanted I must be perfect"), with patients that are addicted ("Everything must go well for me to cope") or with patients with obsessive compulsive disorders ("I must always be perfectly in control to be able to function").

During a critical incident in life (i.e., a stressful life experience), the dysfunctional rule is then activated, resulting in specific errors in thinking, leading to surface level maladaptive thoughts (i.e., I am fat, I can't control my life, I need something to be able to cope).

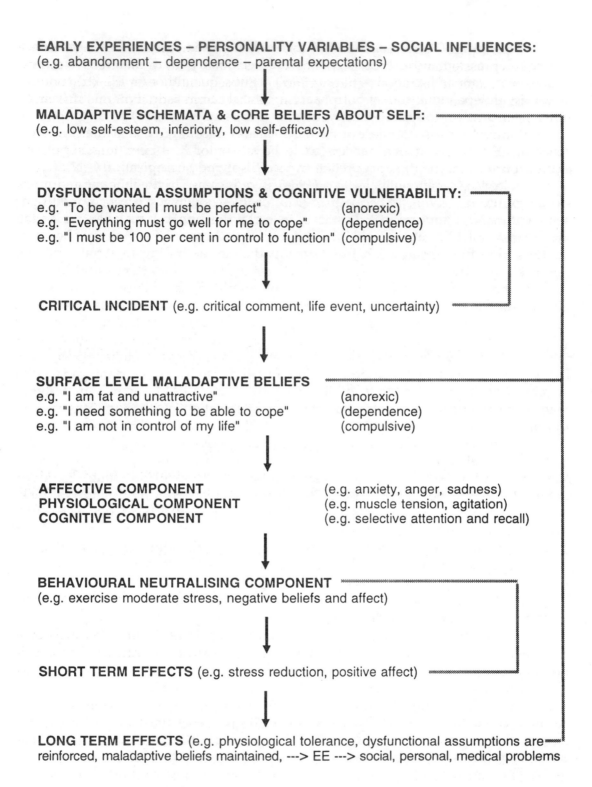

EARLY EXPERIENCES – PERSONALITY VARIABLES – SOCIAL INFLUENCES:
(e.g. abandonment – dependence – parental expectations)

MALADAPTIVE SCHEMATA & CORE BELIEFS ABOUT SELF:
(e.g. low self-esteem, inferiority, low self-efficacy)

DYSFUNCTIONAL ASSUMPTIONS & COGNITIVE VULNERABILITY:
e.g. "To be wanted I must be perfect"   (anorexic)
e.g. "Everything must go well for me to cope"   (dependence)
e.g. "I must be 100 per cent in control to function" (compulsive)

CRITICAL INCIDENT (e.g. critical comment, life event, uncertainty)

SURFACE LEVEL MALADAPTIVE BELIEFS
e.g. "I am fat and unattractive"   (anorexic)
e.g. "I need something to be able to cope"   (dependence)
e.g. "I am not in control of my life"   (compulsive)

AFFECTIVE COMPONENT   (e.g. anxiety, anger, sadness)
PHYSIOLOGICAL COMPONENT   (e.g. muscle tension, agitation)
COGNITIVE COMPONENT   (e.g. selective attention and recall)

BEHAVIOURAL NEUTRALISING COMPONENT
(e.g. exercise moderate stress, negative beliefs and affect)

SHORT TERM EFFECTS (e.g. stress reduction, positive affect)

LONG TERM EFFECTS (e.g. physiological tolerance, dysfunctional assumptions are reinforced, maladaptive beliefs maintained, ---> EE ---> social, personal, medical problems

Table 1. A cognitive behavioural model of excessive exercising

48

These quite distressing thoughts can have a physiological effect (e.g. increase in anxiety, muscle tension, changes in bodily sensations) and/or an affective component (e.g., anger, frustration, guilt, sadness). Subsequently, exercise (behavioural component) serves the function of providing a short-term reduction of stress and a quick feeling of euphoria.

However in the long-term exercise can (a) encourage the patient to avoid confronting the real sources of stress (e.g., dysfunctional assumptions about self, dysfunctional thoughts, inappropriate problem solving strategies);, (b) is likely to lead to tolerance which will lead to a progressive increase in the amount and intensity of exercise; and (c) can become the only problem solving strategy in modifying negative mood. These reinforce and perpetuate the original maladaptive beliefs about one's self.

Methodological issues in assessing excessive exercising

The diagnostic criteria and the questionnaires used in the assessment of EE have varied across studies. This has resulted in some lack of consistency in the research which has been carried out and this has implications for the interpretation of the results. This section will briefly review some of the measures which have been used.

(a) Diagnostic criteria and severity of excessive exercising

Excessive exercising has been associated with physical and psychological risk. This condition is characterized by:

- excessive preoccupation with exercise (Morgan, 1979);

- withdrawal symptoms which could be psychological (feelings of nervousness, guilt, anxiety, lowered self esteem, depression) or physiological (headache, physical discomfort) when restrained from exercising (De Coverley Veale, 1987; Morgan, 1979; Passman and Thompson, 1988);

- continuing to exercise when it is socially or medically contraindicated (Passman and Thompson, 1988);

- loss of other interests and friends, fatigue and neglect of emotional relationships (Robbins and Joseph, 1980).

This provides a useful list of indicators that could alert clinicians suspecting EE. However, there is a scarcity of quantitative measures that can provide cut-off points to differentiate between excessive exercisers and normal exercisers, or measure the degree of excessive exercising.

One way to identify excessive exercisers is to employ the criteria used in the Passman and Thompson (1988) study who administered the Obligatory Exercise Questionnaire (pathological score over 50) and an additional two five-point Likert scales measuring reticence to stop exercising behaviour ("Anxiety following inability to exercise for a period of a week" and "Probability of continuing to exercise following persisting painful injury suffered from exercise"), even though this is not widely established or validated.

There is still a need to establish the specific diagnostic criteria for EE and subsequently refine diagnostic and screening measures to assess severity of EE.

(b) Questionnaires measuring reasons for excessive exercising

Some studies have attempted to show statistical differences between groups of normal and excessive exercisers on questionnaires measuring attitudes to exercise as a way of differentiating the groups (e.g., Commitment to Exercise Scale: Davis et al., 1993; Obligatory Running Scale: Blumenthal et al., 1984; Reasons for Exercise Inventory: Silberstein et al., 1988; Negative Addiction Scale: Hailey and Bailey, 1982; Exercise Dependence Questionnaire, Ogden et al., submitted). As well as helping to identify excessive exercisers, these questionnaires further our understanding of the motivation to exercise.

To derive a more thorough understanding of excessive exercisers' motivation, it is necessary to develop a questionnaire based on dysfunctional thoughts specific to or characteristic of excessive exercising (e.g. about themselves, the exercise behaviour, their motives). This material could be obtained from clinical interviews and from gathering information from other professionals. The aim would be to differentiate between normal and clinical groups on the basis of maladaptive cognitions ("To be a worthy person I must have a perfect shape" or "If I don't exercise I will lose control") as opposed to positive goal-oriented thoughts ("exercise is good for my health" or "exercise makes me a more effective team member"). For example, in clinical groups it has been shown that exercise serves the function of controlling negative mood states (Long et al., 1993) while among college women managing their weight and appearance is a stronger motivator than concerns about health/fitness, stress/mood or social interaction (Cash et al., 1994).

Although questionnaires are useful, there may be some limitations in their use. Questionnaires on EE are also a measure of people's attitudes towards statements describing their own behaviour. Considering the facts that people with eating disorders have a tendency to offer socially desirable rather than truthful responses, and that excessive exercisers seem to share the same narcissistic perfectionism with anorexics, an over reliance on self report measures may not be advisable. Consequently, information processing paradigms that are not so easily open to bias would appear to be particularly useful in EE and AN, as a means of identifying cognitive distortions.

(c) Information processing paradigms in excessive exercising

In examining the role of cognition in EE, there is a need to examine both the content and the process of cognition. It is proposed that the content of thought can be measured using questionnaires. However, the way in which information is selectively processed (i.e., perceived, stored, retrieved) is often seen as an indication of a cognitive deficit, or a method of schema activation that cannot be affected by social desirability effects. It is proposed that data from both questionnaires and information processing measures will add to the understanding of aetiological and maintaining factors in EE and provide a way of testing the proposed cognitive-behavioural model. Two suggested information processing paradigms are:

1. The Stroop Colour Naming task involves asking subjects to name the colour of the ink in which words are written and to ignore the content of the words themselves. However, colour naming of words related to personally or emotionally significant material is significantly impaired. This has been demonstrated in patients with phobia, generalized anxiety disorder, depression, parasuicide, anorexia and bulimia. It is proposed that EE will show impaired processing of shape-related but not food-related words.

2. Delayed Memory Recall task of words, as there is evidence to suggest that recall for emotionally significant material is selectively biased in a wide range of clinical and non-clinical populations. It is proposed that eating disordered patients will show a bias in the recall of food-related words while the excessive exercisers will show a bias in the recall of shape-related words.

Recommendations for research

The above review highlighted the need to conduct further research using both questionnaires and information processing tasks in excessive exercising and eating disorders to improve understanding of EE and the relationship between EE and AN, and to test a cognitive-behavioural model of EE. Consequently, we are currently conducting research with the following aims:

(1) To identify abnormalities in the processing of words related to food, shape and weight in excessive exercisers and patients with eating disorders using the Stroop Colour Naming task and a Delayed Memory Recall task.

(2) To examine similarities or differences between excessive exercise and patients with eating disorders in body dissatisfaction and drive for thinness using questionnaires (Eating Disorders Inventory: Garner and Olmsted, 1984).

(3) To look at the reasons given for engaging in exercise in excessive exercising, using a standardized exercise questionnaire (EDQ: Ogden et al., submitted).

(4) To examine the nature of attitudes towards eating in excessive exercising using measures developed for people with eating disorders.

Clinical implications

A variety of therapeutic approaches have been suggested for use with patients with eating disorders who over-exercise (see Beumont et al., 1994), such as severely restricting activity (Agras and Werne, 1978), response prevention (Mavisskalian, 1982), using self monitoring and a supervised exercise programme (Beumont et al., 1994). Apparently, such treatments seem to focus on the behaviour itself and it is likely that if the key aetiological and mediational factors are not explored treatment will have a short-term effect. However, cognitive-behavioural approaches have also been used providing optimistic results (Long and Hollin, in press).

At a clinical level it is important to identify not only the frequency and intensity of excessive exercising, but also the cognitive, social, emotional, interpersonal and social functions of the behaviour for each individual. More importantly, personality traits, cognitive vulnerabilities and maladaptive schemata need to be explored and challenged using cognitive techniques.

References

Agras, W.S. and Werne, J. (1978). Behaviour therapy in anorexia nervosa: A data based approach to the question. In J.P. Brandy and H.K. Brodie (Eds) *Controversy in psychiatry, Philadelphia: Saund. Press.*

Beck, A.T. (1967). *Depression: Clinical experimental and theoretical aspects.* New York: Harper & Row.

Beck, A.T. (1976). *Cognitive therapy and the emotional disorders*. New York: International University Press.

Beumont, P.J., Arthur, B., Russell, J.D. and Touyz, S.W. (1994). Excessive physical activity in dieting disordered patients: Proposals for a supervised exercise programme. *International Journal of Eating Disorders, 15*, 1, 21-36.

Blumenthal, J.A., O'Toole, L.C. and Chang, J.L. (1984). Is running an analogue to anorexia nervosa? *Journal of the American Medical Association, 252*, 520-523.

Cash, T.F., Novy, P.L. and Grant, J.R. (1994). Why do women exercise? Factor analysis and future validation of the Reasons to Exercise Inventory. *Perceptual and Motor Skills, 78*, 534-544.

Chalmers, J., Catalan, J., Day, A. and Fairburn, C. (1985). Anorexia nervosa presenting as morbid exercising. *Lancet, 1*, 286-287.

Clark, D.M. (1986). A cognitive approach to panic. *Behavioural Research and Therapy, 24*, 461-470.

Davis, C., Brewer, H. and Ratusny. D. (1994). Behavioural frequency and psychological commitment: Necessary concepts in the study of excessive exercising. *Journal of Behavioural Medicine, 16*, 6, 611-628.

De Coverley Veale, D. (1987). Exercise dependence. *British Journal of Addiction, 82*, 541-544.

Eisler, I. and LeGrange, D. (1990). Excessive exercise and anorexia nervosa. *International Journal of Eating Disorders, 9*, 4, 377-386.

Epling, W.F., Pierce W.D. and Stefan, L. (1983) A theory of activity based anorexia. *International Journal of Eating Disorders, 3*, 1, 27-46.

Garner, D.M. and Olmsted, M.P. (1984). *Eating Disorder Inventory: Manual*. Odessa, FL: Psychological Assessment Resources.

Glasser, W. (1976) *Positive addiction*. New York: Harper & Row.

Hailey, B.J. and Bailey, L.A. (1982). Negative addiction in runners: A quantitative approach. *Journal of Sport Behaviour*, 150-154.

Long, C.G. and Hollin. (1995). Assessment and management of eating disordered patients who over-exercise: A four-year follow up of six single case studies. *Journal of Mental Health..*

Long, C.G., Smith, J., Midgley, M. and Cassidy, T. (1993). Over-exercising in anorexic and normal samples: Behaviour and attitudes. *Journal of Mental Health, 2*, 321-327.

Mavisskalian, M. (1982). Anorexia nervosa treated with response prevention and prolonged exposure. *Behavioural Research & Therapy, 20*, 27-31.

Morgan, W. (1979). Negative addiction in runners. *Physical Sports Medicine, 7*, 57-70.

Morris, M., Steinberg, H., Sykes, E.A. and Salmon, P. (1990). Effects of temporary withdrawal from regular running. *Journal of Psychosomatic Research, 34*, 5, 493-500.

Noval, J.D. (1980) Running anorexia (Letter to the editor). *S.A. Medical Journal*, 1024.

Ogden, J., Veale, D. and Summers, Z. (submitted). *The development and validation of the Exercise Dependence Questionnaire* .

Passman, L. and Thompson, J.K. (1988). Body image and eating disturbance in obligatory runners, obligatory weightlifters and sedentary individuals. *International Journal of Eating Disorders, 7*, 759-769.

Pierce, E.F., Daleng, M.L. and McGowan, R.W. (1993). Scores on exercise dependence among dancers. *Perceptual and Motor Skills, 76,* 531-535.

Pierce, E.F., Eastman, N.W., Tripathi, H.L. and Olsen, K.G. (1993). B-Endorphin response to endurance exercise: relationship to exercise dependence. *Perceptual and Motor Skills, 77,* 3, 1, 767-770.

Radovich, P.M., Nash, J.A., Lacy, D.B. and O'Donovan, C. (1989). Effects of low- and high- intensity exercise on plasma and cerebrospinal fluid levels of ir-b-endorphin, ACTH, cortisol, norepinephrine and glucose in the conscious dog. *Brain Research, 498,* 1, 89-98.

Robbins, J.M. and Joseph, P. (1980). *Commitment to running: Implications for family and work.,* Quoted by Morgan, 1979.

Sachs, M. (1981). Running addiction. In M.H. Sachs and M.L.M. Sachs (Eds) *Psychology of running.* Campaign, IL: Human Kinetics Publishers.

Sachs, M.H. (1987). Eating disorders and long distance running. *Integrated Psychiatry, 5,* 201-211.

Salkovskis, P.M. (1985). Obsessional-compulsive problems: A cognitive behavioural analysis. *Behaviour Research and Therapy, 25,* 571-583.

Salkovskis, P.M. and Warwick, H.M.C. (1986). Morbid preoccupations, health anxiety and reassurance: A cognitive behavioural approach to hypochondriasis. *Behavioural Research and Therapy, 24,* 597-602.

Silberstein, L.R., Striegel-Moore, R.H., Timko, C. and Rodin, J. (1988). Behavioural and psychological implications of body dissatisfaction: Do men and women differ? *Sex Roles, 19,* 219-232.

Slade, P. (1982). Towards a functional analysis of anorexia nervosa and bulimia nervosa. *British Journal of Clinical Psychology, 21,* 3, 167-179.

Sours, J.A. (1980). *Starving to death in a sea of objects: The anorexia nervosa syndrome.* New York: Jason Aronson.

Steptoe, A. and Bolton, J. (1988). The short term influence of high and low intensity physical exercise on mood. *Psychology and Health, 2,* 91-106.

Steptoe, A. and Cox, S. (1988). Acute effects of aerobic exercise on mood. *Health Psychology, 7,* 329-340.

Yates, A. Leehey, K. and Shisslak, C.M. (1983). Running - an analogue of anorexia? *New England Journal of Medicine, 308,* 251-255.

8

Video Interviews: "Hooked" on Exercise

Rhonda Cohen

The March (1995) issue of *The Psychologist* discussed the relative merits and drawbacks of qualitative research. The fact that a BPS journal should devote an entire issue to this method of research is indicative of psychology becoming more receptive to the different concepts of "data" and "fact" which qualitative research employs. However, today both methods are more likely to be recognized as having equal value in providing insight into psychological matters and so it becomes more of a decision for the researcher to choose between methods according to the requirements of the work in hand. In the present study, it was decided to utilize two psychological research methods which might be viewed as more qualitative, i.e. case study and interview techniques. This research includes a nine-minute filmed interview of two subjects heavily involved in sport and exercise. A discussion on the advantages and disadvantages of the case study methods begins this paper, followed by a brief case study of the subjects.

The case study as a method

A case study gives comprehensive and detailed information about an individual or group. Usually, this incorporates an extensive history, often gained through an interview. It offers facts about the person's employment, education, and family background, and may contain an expansive account of experiences important to the inquiry which makes the case of notable interest. In the present case studies the subjects are interesting because of the extent to which sport/exercise is involved in their lives.

An advantage of a qualitative case study is its usefulness in exposing broad psychological issues such as the influences of heredity versus environment in sport as well as the interaction of physiological and psychological aspects of addiction. From this wealth of detailed information common factors may be extracted. A quantitative study may then be pursued in an attempt to link the variables which have surfaced. For example, a qualitative case study could suggest links to be explored between sports addiction and an overbearing authoritative influence from parents and coaches, which a quantitative study could then further determine.

Another advantage of the case study is the possibility that an extraordinary case may arise which would not be noticed in a pre-planned study. In sport where those who exercise have quite complex lifestyles and manipulate circumstances in a variety of ways, the case study could reveal factors which may otherwise be missed, and which may form the basis for new theories to emerge.

Evidence may arise from a case study which is contradictory in nature, and such challenges to extant theory can promote new and valuable research. In exercise and sport, the athlete that doesn't fit into the mould of psychiatric patient may still have psychological problems or histories which challenge more physiologically-based sport addiction theories.

Case studies are often criticized as being rather unscientific, and also for the limitation of their lack of generalization. Though this is an obvious disadvantage, the richness of a case study can provide the foundations for much further quantitative research (Bromley, 1986).

The retrospective aspect of subjects' reports in case study method is also often criticized as being unreliable. However, this can be overcome through the validation of evidence confirmed from others involved in the subjects' lives. Bromley (1986) states that although case studies are also difficult to replicate, this disadvantage is compensated for by the richness and quality of information elicited by this method. He also believes that a preoccupation with experiments and psychometrics has meant a negligence and devaluation of the case study method, which in spite of the disadvantages mentioned above can still be significant and useful.

Whilst the following case studies can be criticized for all the reasons listed, it is believed that they also carry all of the advantages of studies of their kind. It is to be hoped that they provide many possibilities for further research.

Method

The design was an informal introductory interview, followed by a gathering of information for the brief case study, and finishing with a more formal filmed interview.

The subjects were selected from a small sample of people working at Barnet College who are all heavily involved in sport and or exercise. The first subject is a 24-year-old male, referred to as LB, while the second subject is a 36-year-old female, designated RM. They were chosen because of the extent to which they exercise both daily and weekly, as well as for the way in which they have manipulated their lives to fit around their exercise. The subjects agreed to be filmed, though wished their names to remain confidential. More details on the subjects are given in the case study section.

The materials used were questions broadly based on the Ogden et al. (1995) Dependency Questionnaire. The questions were put into broad categories from which it was hoped that the subjects' answers would lead back to similar more specific questions found in the questionnaire. (See appendix for a sample of interview questions.)

The procedure

Prior to filming

Ten subjects were interviewed initially through an informal chat about what exercise they were involved in and how often they engaged in these activities. In the second meeting, questions became more formalized in a pre-video conversation where the interviewer took notes on sport/exercise schedules and patterns. After that session, the interviewer broached the subject of a taped interview and invited the subjects to participate in the filming. Four subjects agreed to be filmed, from whom two were chosen.

In the studio

The filming of the video was done in a college media studio. Video cameras were kept as unobtrusive as possible and the interviewer and subjects were able to sit for 15 minutes and chat before filming. A table was placed between the interviewer and subject. It was hot under the lights but all present felt that the time went very quickly. The interviewer had questions in front of her and the interviewee had already been briefed as to what questions to expect. Of course, in the spirit of freeflow conversation not all questions nor answers were pre-rehearsed. A live video camera in the room may have dominated the room, yet it was hoped that the informal chatty atmosphere presented by the interviewer with a loosely structured open-ended interview would keep the subjects relaxed.

During the filming

At the start of the taped interview, questions to do with exercise and patterns were asked in order to acclimatise the subjects to the studio setting. The language that was used was neither formal nor psychological in nature. The term "addiction" was avoided and the words being "dependent" or "hooked" on exercise were substituted, because of the negative connotations that the word "addiction" may possess. The interviewer tried to remain non-judgmental, by merely asking questions rather that summarizing or commenting.

Editing

Thirteen minutes of raw interview footage was filmed and then cut down to nine minutes of tape, including titles and credits. Finally the taped interview was edited. The researcher was subjective in selecting certain aspects of the conversation. Information regarding exercise and exercise routine was paramount and thus other important aspects of the person's life, though interesting, may have been neglected. Scenes of the subjects performing their exercise were also filmed and interspersed throughout the video.

Case study 1: LB

LB is a young man of 24 who exercises regularly. His weekly pattern is a repetitive one in which he alternates weight training, aerobics, cycling and step aerobics with running. He exercises three hours a day on average. In addition he works out for four hours a week as part of a football team. This involves an additional two nights of training plus a Sunday game. As a child LB was strongly encouraged to play football after school by his parents. He felt that he was good at this activity and enjoyed the approval from his parents for his adeptness. Playing sport was always a part of his life and his whole week revolved around it. LB left school to pursue A levels at an FE college. He chose to undertake the sport studies programme which involved taking two A levels as well as a City & Guilds Certificate in Coaching, leadership bronze medal, and sport injury certification. LB worked hard and was a conscientious student. He participated in many sport activities offered by the college in his free time between classes. He was successful on all accounts and passed the sport studies exam with a grade B. LB decided to pursue a degree in sports studies at university only to drop out after the first year. He felt that the HE course was too general as well as repetitive of the A level and he wanted something different. He expressed an interest in a career in PE education, or a degree in exercise physiology.

LB got a part-time job at the college after leaving higher education. Most of his hours are spent training and teaching others sport and so he actually spends even more time with sport than his designated three hours of exercise. He feels that his job fits into his exercise and enjoys the time he spends both at work and at leisure. LB feels lucky to be working part-time so that his life can revolve around exercise. When asked whether he could ever foresee working in a nine-to-five office job and pushing sport aside, he replied simply "no". He says that sport will always be his life and he'd rather work part-time and earn less in a sport-related job than work full-time in a business setting with a salary twice as high.

LB lives to exercise at work, after work, and during holidays. In the summer he often goes abroad for three months to play football and to work out. He admits that he manipulates it this way so that he can be very active all summer. LB wouldn't go anywhere where this daily routine would be impossible. He says that it hasn't interfered with his relationships so far as the girls he has been involved in were also sporty. LB says that perhaps it could interfere with his life in the future, but for now, only an injury would cause an imbalance as it would depress him greatly.

Case study 2: RM

RM is a 36-year-old woman with a partner and two children. She currently both runs 35 miles and cycles 10 miles weekly. RM started swimming four or five times a week from the age of eight. Her father encouraged her to swim as he had been a competitive swimmer when he was younger and coached at a local swimming club. The family actively pursued the outdoor life and she was brought up camping, walking and cycling. At 12 years old she became fed up with swimming, though continued to exercise daily. Her mother died that same year of cancer.

At 14 years of age, she was required to participate in cross-country runs at school. She did well and was asked to represent her school on the team. Inter-school sports were highly regarded at her school and she was proud to participate. She was also motivated by the fact that most of the students who went on "away" visits to other schools were male and as she was a pubescent teen, this also was one of her prime reasons. RM played on the school's hockey and cricket B teams. As a teenager she also began to realize that running could be a real outlet for pent-up emotions. She felt that she received a lot of approval from her coach about the level of her fitness and weight and that her being slim and eating less was a reinforcing thing. The less she ate, the more positive reinforcement she got from her coach and the better she then felt about herself.

During the first year of RM's social work degree, her father died of cancer. She felt that she was able to handle the pressure of this through her running. She remembers how she went for a very long run upon the news of his death. She ran even though it was midnight and continued until she couldn't go any further. The only thing that ever got in the way of her running was an occasional injury which meant that she needed to resort to more sedate exercises instead.

In 1983 RM decided to travel around Europe. She said that she took her running shoes everywhere. She waitressed part-time in Scotland and went running every afternoon in the hills. RM moved to London to take up a part-time social work post. There she joined a running club in Islington. Running became an escape from what she describes as a shabby bedsit. RM says that she spent all her free time at the running club just to avoid going home. She became involved in competitive running, including marathons, and this was how she met her partner.

Of primary concern to RM was always the need to improve her running time and to stay slim. An unplanned pregnancy threw her plans astray although she carried on running up to the time her daughter was born, which was four weeks earlier than her due date. She liked being a mum but couldn't wait to go back to her running.* RM used to go to the park and leave the pram in the centre while she ran laps around it. She got fit quickly so that she could return to competitive racing. Before every race she says she would breast feed to relieve herself of the weight of milk that made running very difficult. Sometimes she would run to the club and half way back she would meet her partner. He would hand over the buggy and she would then proceed to push it home while her partner would run to the club and back. This was the equitable way they had both worked out to have an equi-distant run.

Now RM cycles to work, runs at lunch times, cycles home, and then runs in the evenings. She looks forward to races on the weekends and often runs to the park to meet the family there for a picnic. She feels that she definitely manipulates holidays and summers to fit in to her running. She'll run in all weather, though she says that it's hard to run in snow. RM says that she needs to run and will probably run, barring injury, even as a granny.

Discussion

A filmed interview is quite an unnatural situation. Yet in this study it was vital that subjects felt relaxed enough to reveal intimate information, and so a sense of intimacy had to be created. This was built up through the use of pre-video conversations which could be argued to have interfered with the interviewer's objectivity. Nevertheless, the subjects were encouraged to speak freely and their answers were unrestricted by carefully asking open-ended questions.

It is interesting to note that, initially, neither subject realized the extent to which sport/exercise was essential in their lives. Yet it was quite apparent how they both manipulated holidays, summers, relationships and daily routines to fit into their sport/exercise patterns. Sport/exercise is a part of their lives and they cannot imagine feeling well without it. Both can only perceive their futures with sport/exercise continuing to play a major role.

---

* An American "baby jogger" is advertised by Racing Strollers Inc. – a pram with big wheels which apparently can be jogged anywhere, even over cobblestones.

There appears to be a relationship between sport and self-image in the case of RM, as well as a link between sport/exercise and her perception of her weight. In the case of LB, there appears to be an association between sport/exercise and his self worth and the need to achieve. This dependency on sport/exercise could have developed as a compensatory behaviour for the over-bearing and domineering family environment from which both subjects emerge. These attitudes and behaviours towards sport/behaviour may have been further reinforced by their coaches.

The interviewer found that using a filmed interview, as part of a case study, has been a useful tool in studying sport/exercise addiction and has highlighted the issues of self-worth, self-image, weight control and families. The issues that have been raised provide discussion points for the further development of addiction theories.

Acknowledgement

I gratefully acknowledge the help of Juan Cruz in the editing of the video tape.*

References

Bromley, D.B. (1986). *The case study method in psychology and related disciplines*. Chichester: Wiley.

Coolican, H. (1994). *Research methods and statistics in psychology*. London: Hodder & Stoughton.

Henwood, K.L. and Pidgeon, N.F. (1992). Qualitative research and psychological testing. *British Journal of Psychology, 83*, 83-111.

Henwood K.L. and Pidgeon N.F. (1995). Grounded theory and psychological research . *The Psychologist, 8, 3*, 115-118.

Ogden, J., Veale, D. and Summers, Z. (submitted) The Development and Validation of the Exercise Dependence Questionnaire.

Skinner, B.F. (1956). A case history in the scientific method. *The American Psychologist, 11*, 221-223.

---

* More information about the video can be obtained from Rhonda Cohen at Barnet College.

Appendix

General format of questions used

1   Thanks for agreeing to this interview. I know that you are very involved in exercise from a work as well as social position, so I'd like to talk to you about how much exercise you undertake.

2   Firstly, what type of exercise do you do?

3   Do you have a certain pattern of exercise? How many hours a week does this involve?

4   When do you exercise? How do you fit it into your life?

5   Why do you exercise?

6   How do you feel if you don't exercise?

7   Do you feel that there is a relationship between your exercise/sport and your moods?

8   Does exercise give you a high?

9   Does exercise ever interfere with your life? Control your life?

10   Would you like to do more/less?

11   Have you ever gone to any extremes? Summers or holidays?

12   Would you say that you are hooked (or dependent) on exercise?

13   Do you feel that your eating problems were linked with your sport?

14   How did you manage to exercise while you were pregnant?

Mood States, Menstrual Cycle and Exercise-to-Music

I.M. Cockerill, S.L. Lawson and A.M. Nevill

Within recent years there has been a considerable increase in the number of women participating in regular, intensive exercise, both for preparing for competitive sport and for fitness and general wellbeing. It is now well established that exercising aerobically four times a week for at least 20 minutes can produce a beneficial physiological training effect, together with the concomitant psychological bonus of increased vigour and general positive affect (Greist, 1978; Plummer and Koh, 1987; McGowan, 1991; Maroulakis and Zervas, 1993). Indeed, Thayer (1989) has argued that exercise is the most natural way of modulating mood and the medical profession is increasingly prescribing regular exercise as an antidote to depression, although it is not clear how such recommendations are defined either qualitatively or quantitatively.

The popularity of distance running, which coincided with the so-called marathon boom, has waned and at the present time perhaps the most popular form of aerobic exercise for non-competitive participants is exercise-to-music – known variously as aerobics, popmobility, and step – and progressive-resistance training using either free weights or exercise machines of various kinds. However, running remains a relatively widespread form of exercise and has led to the greatest number of studies which have examined the relationship between aerobic running and psychological mood. Early work by Nowlis and Greenberg (1979) found that mood enhancement occurred following a 12.5 miles run. Such studies, however, tend to vary quite markedly in their design, some with very few participants and most measuring mood before and after a period of exercise, at best.

Few studies have investigated the extent to which it is possible to overdo exercise, leading not only to a risk of injury to muscles and joints, but also to a high level of fatigue which eradicates any beneficial effect from regular exercise. In other words, exercise may be good for you, but how much exercise? Gondola and Tuckman (1983) found that positive mood profiles, as measured by the POMS questionnaire (McNair et al., 1971), were produced by athletes running an average of 24 miles per week, whereas a group of marathon runners showed a negative profile. Cockerill et al. (1992) subsequently suggested that there may be an optimal range of miles run per week that will facilitate a positive mood state, while exceeding, say,

50 miles per week can have the opposite effect. It is also important to consider Ullyot's (1986) suggestion that the frequency, intensity, duration, and mode of running needs to be taken into account before specific claims can be made as to its benefit, or otherwise.

Literature associated with the effects of the highly popular exercise-to-music on psychological wellbeing is relatively meagre, despite the fact that it has been reported by Lawrence (1987) that in the United States some 20 million people participate. It remains much more popular with women than with men and is marketed on the basis of its beneficial effects upon body shape, self-concept, and positive mood. Specific evidence in support of such claims was difficult to find. Frazier and Nagy (1988), having measured mood among women before and after a 15-week aerobics programme, concluded that there was no evidence of mood change. By contrast, Maroulakis and Zervas (1993) measured the moods of female aerobics participants just before and immediately after a class, with a follow-up 24 hours later. They found that exercise appeared to enhance mood and that its effects remained at re-test, thereby supporting an earlier study by Barabasz (1991). Altogether studies of the effects of aerobic exercise on mood has yielded equivocal results, due largely to variations in the design of the investigations, some examining short-term effects and some long-term, some having a control group and some not, while the numbers of participants has also tended to vary, from groups containing fewer than ten participants to up to four times that number.

A critical variable to consider when studying the effects of exercise on mood states is the menstrual cycle. Once again, both physiological and psychological aspects need to be considered, especially when set against the available evidence suggesting that at least 50 per cent of menstruating women experience some form of dysmenorrhea, while high levels of prostaglandin at menstruation can cause nausea, headache, backache and muscle cramp. It has also been shown by Cockerill et al. (1992) that even among regular exercisers mood becomes increasingly negative during the few days before menstruation. Accordingly, evidence to suggest that regular, intensive exercise alleviates both dysmenorrhea and negative mood remains equivocal and, although exercise can facilitate both physiological and psychological states, it has been suggested by O'Brien (1989) that too much exercise may cause menstrual abnormalities, which begs the question, how much is too much? What is becoming increasingly apparent is that daily, strenuous exercise which occupies more than two hours is likely to cause some form of menstrual dysfunction.

Oral contraception plays an important role in the lives of many women of child-bearing age and it is appropriate to be aware of this factor when designing a study which manipulates the menstrual cycle as an independent variable. However, the significance of oral contraceptive use among athletes may be overemphasized in the light of Wells' (1985) finding that only between five and 12 per cent of athletes use oral contraception. This observation may be associated with a belief held by some athletes their that performance will be limited if artificial means of menstrual-cycle control are used.

The purpose of the present experiment was to examine the psychological effects of regular, intensive aerobic activity, in the form of exercise-to-music classes, upon the moods of women who participated at different levels of frequency, while taking into account associated menstrual cycles. It was hypothesized that regular, moderate to intensive exercise is psychologically beneficial; that general criteria can be established for the frequency and intensity of exercise, above and below which the activity will not yield a mood-enhancing effect; and that exercise has a mediating effect upon menstrual cycle symptoms.

Method

Participants

Fifty-four women aged between 18 and 38 years (mean age = 22.1 years) participated in the study, of whom 42 were enrolled in exercise-to-music classes at the University of Birmingham. A further 12 women, who were also students at Birmingham, did not take any form of exercise and they constituted the control group. All participants were volunteers. According to the number of hourly classes taken each week, each of the 42 exercisers was allocated to one of three groups; more than four classes, between two and three, and one. The numbers per group and those using oral contraception are shown in Table 1.

Table 1. Participants according to amount of exercise per week, regularity of menstruation and oral contraceptive use

Amount of exercise	4+ times/week	2-3 times/week	Once per week	None
Number of participants	12	17	13	12
Oral contraceptive used	5	10	8	6
Amenorrhoeic	2	0	2	0

Apparatus

The Profile of Mood States Questionnaire (POMS) was used to evaluate mood state using a "right now" response (McNair et al., 1971). The Moos (1968) Menstrual Distress Questionnaire was also completed by participants. It was renamed the Body Awareness Questionnaire (Cockerill et al., 1994) to minimize bias towards negative responding, although Markum (1976) found that knowing the purpose of the questionnaire using neutral instructions did not affect ratings for the eight menstrual symptoms evaluated.

Design

A six-week diary was used by the exercising groups to record the days of their classes. All participants completed two POMS questionnaires each week after an exercise class, if appropriate, and at least two hours after exercise. The procedure was repeated 72 hours later at a similar time of day and extended over a six-week duration. This timing meant that the follicular-ovulatory, luteal, and menstrual phases of the cycle could be monitored for mood variation among participants. Two POMS questionnaires were completed within 72 hours so that responses recorded during menstruation, for example, would not suggest that mood at menstruation was being monitored specifically. One questionnaire per week may not have coincided with all three phases, resulting in an incomplete data set. Those taking one class each week did the second POMS 72 hours after the first, while the non-exercisers completed the questionnaires over a 72-hour interval on similar days of the week over the six weeks. Days of POMS completion were shown by the letter 'P'.

Three Body Awareness Questionnaires (BAQ) were completed, one at each stage of the cycle as far as this could be determined. For example, the first BAQ was on the second day of menstruation, the second exactly 14 days later, and the third two days before their next period was anticipated. Amenorrhoeic women completed a BAQ at two-week intervals on a similar day each fortnight for the duration of the study. Thus, questionnaire completion by amenorrhoeic women provided a control to monitor mood changes or physiological distress that might reasonably be attributed to menstrual cycle effects. Finally, BAQ completion was denoted by a 'B' in the diary, while days of menstruation were asterisked. This information was used to determine the questionnaire responses that were applicable to each phase of the cycle.

Procedure

All participants were volunteers who had responded either to posters located in the University sports centre, or to requests for volunteers made during exercise classes. Demographic data were obtained and, in addition, two POMS inventories, one BAQ and a diary were issued during the first week of the study, at the end of which they were collected and two further POMS inventories issued. The initial BAQ was completed during the menstrual phase and upon handing this in a second BAQ was given, to be completed 14 days later. This procedure was repeated for the duration of the study. All participants were informed that the data they provided would remain confidential and that they could withdraw from the study at any time without giving a reason for doing so. At the end of the six weeks all participants were told the precise nature of the research.

Results

The two combined POMS measures in each of weeks one, three and six are represented as mean mood profiles in Figures 1, 2, and 3, respectively.

A multivariate analysis of variance (MANOVA) was conducted on the data. Figure 1 shows that in week one all four groups displayed similar levels of depression, anger and vigour ($p > 0.05$). However, significant differences were found between groups for the three remaining factors of tension, fatigue and confusion, while differences between the four groups for confusion varied significantly for both mood measurements recorded during week one ($p < 0.01$). The mean confusion score for the controls was significantly ($p < 0.01$) higher (mean=11.92) than the combined score for the exercisers (mean=7.9).

As can be seen in Figure 2, by the third week the exercise programme appeared to be having a positive effect upon all three exercising groups irrespective of amount of activity per week. The two more active groups were displaying the clear-

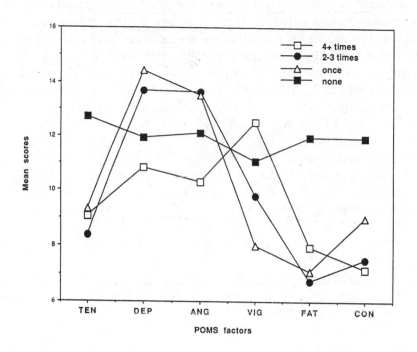

Figure 1. Mood profiles for each group – week 1

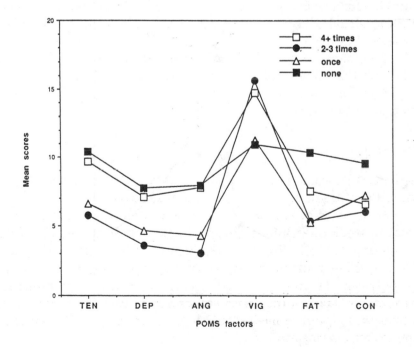

Figure 2. Mood profiles for each group – week 3

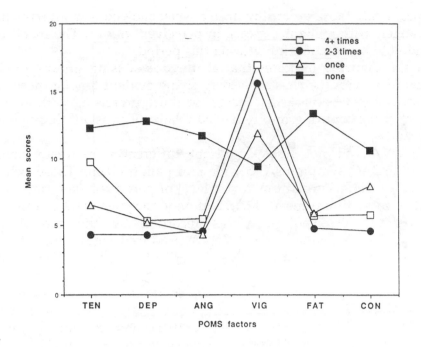

Figure 3. Mood profiles for each group – week 6

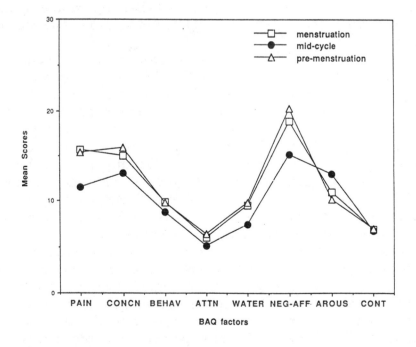

Figure 4. Mean BAQ scores at each of three menstrual cycle phases

est iceberg profiles, while those exercising once a week showed a small reduction in depression and anger, with a slight increase in perceived vigour. The mood of the control group did not vary significantly during this period.

By week six, Figure 3 indicates that all three exercising groups produced positive mood profiles, with the clearest iceberg shape evident among those taking four or more classes and less-marked icebergs for those exercising with lower frequency. The mood of the control group remained relatively constant throughout the six weeks of the study.

The MANOVA did not find significant differences between exercising groups on any of the BAQ symptoms, other than for pain ($p < 0.05$). Those exercising two or three times a week recorded the lowest level of perceived pain (mean=12.2), followed by four or more times (mean=12.2), and only once per week (mean=14.26). The highest level of perceived pain was recorded by the control group (mean=17.14). On the other hand, the MANOVA produced significant differences over the three phases of the menstrual cycle for all BAQ symptoms. These data are shown in Figure 4.

BAQ scores recorded at the mid-cycle phase were clearly lower for six of the eight symptoms of the Body Awareness Questionnaire ($p < 0.01$). The two exceptions were arousal, which was significantly higher ($p < 0.01$), and control, where there were non-significant differences between menstrual cycle phases ($p > 0.10$).

Discussion

In general, the data showed that the inactive women felt more tense, depressed and less vigorous than those in the exercising groups, which supports the opinion of Thayer (1989), among others, that regular participation in vigorous exercise may be an analogue of psychological wellbeing.

Some of those participating in the study were returning to regular exercise following several weeks of relative inactivity, while others were beginning exercise classes for the first time. Thus, it can be stated with reasonable confidence that each participant was evaluated from a baseline of little or no exercise for the previous three months. At the end of week one the non-exercisers' mood scores varied very little between each of the six factors (Figure 1), while those exercising more than four times a week appeared to be benefiting psychologically from their multiple sessions; they were already beginning to show the well-known iceberg profile with high vigour and low scores on the five negative factors. These data suggest that the claim by Barabasz (1991) and Maroulakis and Zervas (1993) that a single bout of aerobic exercise is sufficient to enhance mood may be premature.

By the end of the third week a clear iceberg profile was emerging for each exercise group, but the non-exercisers profile remained psychologically similar to that in week one. Figure 2 shows that more than a single hour of exercise per week is required if mood enhancement is to occur as a consequence of that exercise. Moreover, Figure 3 suggests that more than four classes a week may be too much for some women, especially after a layoff, since the tension, depression and anger scores of the high-frequency participants were higher than for both the other exercising groups, and was very similar to those for the non-exercisers.

The most dramatic contrast among group profiles is revealed in Figure 3, with clear iceberg profiles for the exercisers, but a much flatter outline for the non-exercise group. A closer inspection of each individual mood factor shows that the best profile was for those who exercised between two and three times a week. They were less tense, depressed, and confused than any of the other participants. This graph also reveals that the high-frequency exercise group was more tense and confused than the other exercisers. These data are contrary to those of Frazier and Nagy (1988), which showed that a 15-week programme of aerobics did not produce a change in mood.

However, as pointed out earlier, there is a tendency among some exercisers to overdo this activity, which may lead to negative, rather than positive, affect. While it is unlikely that a single hour of exercise-to-music will lead to severe over-training and ultimate burnout, as defined by Smith (1986) and Schmidt and Stein (1991), there was some evidence that by week six those who participated in more than four classes a week appeared to be less well adjusted psychologically than the two to three times a week group.

Of course, it is always difficult to extrapolate wholly meaningful results from mood data generated by post-menarchal and pre-menopausal females, since the potential confounding variable of menstrual-cycle phase is always likely to have an influence upon the data. The present study attempted to control for such effects by requiring participants to complete their POMS questionnaires at various stages of the cycle, while disguising the fact that menstrual-cycle effects were to be an aspect of the experimental design. The Body Awareness Questionnaire (BAQ) data showed that there was a significant variation in overall scores at the three stages of the cycle (Figure 4). The well-known dysmenorrheic symptoms experienced by many women during menstruation, and the more equivocal, yet much-reported, evidence for the existence of pre-menstrual syndrome, are supported by the very similar scores produced at the menstrual and pre-menstrual phases. However, a menstrual-phase effect was only significant for pain and arousal. At mid-cycle all participants experienced less pain and greater positive affect. The scores for control were extremely similar, which suggests that the BAQ was being answered honestly, since this factor is included as a control for social desirability and scores should always be randomly distributed among respondents if each is answering honestly.

Although there was no evidence that amount of exercise had a significant effect upon BAQ scores, the number of participants within each group was fairly small and a replication with greater numbers may produce somewhat different results. Accordingly, the women who were amenorrheic and those who used oral contraception were too few to be analysed separately, although these are important variables to control in a subsequent study. It can be concluded that the present data offer further support for the physiological and psychological benefits of regular, vigorous aerobic exercise. By monitoring mood state on a regular basis it should be possible to use that information as a guide to exercise prescription, as well as a safeguard against the effects of overtraining and associated negative effects of excessive exercise.

References

Barabasz M. (1991). Effects of aerobic exercise on transient mood state. *Perceptual and Motor Skills, 73,* 657-658.

Cockerill I.M., Nevill, A.M. and Byrne, N.J. (1992). Mood, mileage and the menstrual cycle. *British Journal of Sports Medicine, 26,* 145-150.

Cockerill I.M., Wormington, J.A. and Nevill, A.M. (1994). Menstrual-cycle effects on mood and perceptual-motor performance. *Journal of Psychosomatic Research, 38,* 763-771.

Cox, D.J. (1983). Menstrual symptoms in college students: A controlled study. *Journal of Behavioural Medicine, 6,* 335-338.

Frazier, S.E. and Nagy, S. (1988). Mood-state changes of women as a function of regular aerobic exercise. *Perceptual and Motor Skills, 68,* 283-287.

Gondola, J.C. and Tuckman, B.W. (1983). Extent of training and mood enhancement in women runners. *Perceptual and Motor Skills, 57,* 333-334.

Greist, J.H. (1978). Running through your mind. *Journal of Psychosomatic Research, 22,* 259-294.

Lawrence, K. (1987). Mainstreaming men into aerobics. *Fitness Management, 3,* 23-24.

McGowan, R.W., Pierce, E.F. and Jordan, D. (1991). Mood alterations with a single bout of physical activity. *Perceptual and Motor Skills, 72,* 1203-1209.

McNair, D.M., Lorr, M. and Droppleman, L.F. (1971). *Manual for the profile of mood states.* San Diego, CA: Educational and Industrial Testing Service.

Markum, R.A. (1976). Assessment of the reliablity of and the effect of neutral instructions on the symptom ratings on the Moos Menstrual Distress Questionnaire. *Psychosomatic Medicine, 38,* 163-172.

Maroulakis, M. and Zervas, Y. (1993). Effects of aerobic exercise on mood of adult women. *Perceptual and Motor Skills, 76,* 795-801.

Moos, R.H. (1968). The development of a menstrual-distress questionnaire. *Psychosomatic Medicine, 30,* 853-867.

Nowlis, D.P. and Greenberg, N. (1979). Empirical description of effects of exercise on mood. *Perceptual and Motor Skills, 49,* 1001-1002.

O'Brien, M. (1989). The effects of exercise on the menstrual cycle. *Cinesiologie, 127,* 274-276.

Plummer, O.K. and Koh, K.O. (1987). Effect of aerobics on self-concepts of college women. *Perceptual and Motor Skills, 65,* 271-275.

Schmidt, G.W. and Stein, G.L. (1991). Sport commitment: A model integrating enjoyment, dropout and burnout. *Journal of Sport and Exercise Psychology, 8,* 254-265.

Smith, R.E. (1986). Toward a cognitive-affective model of athletic burnout. *Journal of Sport Psychology, 8,* 36-50.

Thayer, R.E. (1987). *The biophysiology of mood and arousal.* Oxford University Press.

Ullyott, J. (1981). Amenorrhea: A sensitive subject. *Womens Sports,* (December), 46-47.

Wells, C.L. (1985) *Women, sport and performance: A physiological perspective.* Champaign, Illinois: Human Kinetics.

10

Summing up

John Annett

A workshop provides an excellent opportunity to review work in progress, to report informal observations and to discuss ideas which have not yet gained the unequivocal acceptance of the scientific community. In the course of a very interesting day we have had contributions in all of these categories.

Sewell and his colleagues reported a comparative study of golfers and runners with the finding that the anticipation of exercise elevated the mood of golfers but only the runners felt better afterwards. At least on the measures used in this study there appears to be no common pattern in the relationship between exercise and mood in "addicts" of these two sports.

Cockerill and his colleagues, using different subjective measures of mood, reported positive effects of moderate amounts of exercise to music on mood and menstrual cycle affect in women, but these results may not be strictly relevant to the question of addiction.

Cohen presented two brief case studies on video which exemplify the concept of exercise addiction as it is generally understood, but should we find it strange that a young man can spend 18 hours a week or more exercising or a young mother takes her new baby jogging in the park? These are surely but mild eccentricities, comparable with those exhibited by individuals who spend their spare time pretending to be Elvis Presley or in playing Scrabble.

The case studies presented by Seheult and Cripps, further illustrate the multifaceted character of exercise addiction.

Veale, using the preferred term "exercise dependence", doubts whether such a syndrome actually exists as a clinical entity, except possibly as one manifestation of an eating disorder in some individuals, and is proposing in-depth investigation of all the relevant aspects of exercise motivation to clarify the issues.

The approach of Loumidis and Roxborough is similarly guided by clinical caution. Hall also advises a more detailed understanding of the variety of factors which contribute to the motivation of the regular exerciser and draws attention to the possible role of imagery in the self-motivation of élite athletes. During the workshop it became clear that there is a danger of confusing exercise adherence with exercise dependence and exercise addiction. The term "addiction" is strictly used in relation to physiological adaptation to drugs but has been extended to other varieties of apparently obsessional behaviour for which there is no known physiological basis.

Steinberg et al. remind us that the hypothesis that exercise releases endorphins giving rise to the symptoms of the "runner's high" and to physiological dependence remains no more than a hypothesis for which there is some supportive, but by no means conclusive, evidence. Criteria for true addiction based on endorphin release should include not only direct physiological evidence but also that effects should be pleasurable, the activity should be truly compulsive, the pain threshold should be raised, withdrawal symptoms should occur, opiate antagonists should be effective and there should be an acquired tolerance.

If the workshop has one message for newcomers to sports psychology, it is that attractive and popular ideas, like exercise addiction, turn out to be more complex than at first sight and that there is no substitute for systematic investigation based on clear thinking.

Motivation for Participation
in Sport and Exercise

Edited by

John Annett

Barry Cripps

and

Hannah Steinberg

An occasional paper for the Sport and Exercise Psychology Section of
The British Psychological Society, based on proceedings
of a one-day workshop at Warwick University.

APR96

Published by The British Psychological Society
St Andrews House, 48 Princess Road East, Leicester LE1 7DR

© 1995 The British Psychological Society

ISBN 1 85433 2015